DANCER TO DANCER

By Melissa Hayden

MELISSA HAYDEN: OFFSTAGE AND ON

DANCER TO DANCER

Advice for Today's Dancer

MELISSA HAYDEN

1981   ANCHOR PRESS/DOUBLEDAY   Garden City, New York

Dancer to Dancer: Advice for Today's Dancer is published simultane-ously in hardcover and paperback editions.

Anchor Books Edition: 1981

Designed by Sylvia DeMonte-Bayard

All photographs by Carolyn George except pp. 5, 11, 185; pp. 8, 80 by Martha Swope; p. 79 © Greek Photo News; p. 173 by Frank Derbas; and p. 197 by George Goodwin.

Hardcover Edition
ISBN: 0-385-15582-4
Paperback Edition
ISBN: 0-385-15550-6
Library of Congress Catalog Card Number 80–940
Copyright © 1981 by Melissa Hayden

To Jennifer and Stuart

ACKNOWLEDGMENTS

It would be impossible to acknowledge all the people—teachers, dancers, choreographers, friends, and family—who contributed to the knowledge I acquired during my career as a dancer and a teacher. I can thank some of the individuals who helped make this book possible, however: Jerry Bywaters Cochran; Doris Hering and Nicholas Grimaldi of the National Association for Regional Ballet; all my students, who are represented in this book by Heather Hughes, Alison Gonzalez, and Paula Hughes; my daughter, Jennifer, who contributed many young dancer's insights; my son, Stuart; my husband, Donald Coleman; and my colleagues at Melissa Hayden, Inc., Wilhelm Burmann and Alfonso Catá. Last, but not least, I thank our friend, Paul Epstein, who helped to turn the idea for this book from talk to reality and introduced me to my co-worker, Joyce Christmas, who enabled me to get the words on paper to share what I have learned with all young dancers.

CONTENTS

DANCER TO DANCER

PART I

Becoming a Dancer

1

THE DESIRE
TO DANCE

I couldn't live without dancing.

If I had never had the opportunity to discover that I could dance—that I wanted to dance more than anything—I know I would have been a different person, and I believe that I would not have had the happiness that my life has given me.

If I hadn't discovered dance (at the comparatively late age of fifteen), I would not have enjoyed the unique experience in self-discovery that dancing provides. Yet it sometimes seems like pure accident that I began to study ballet at all. I remember that I was restless, confused about who I was and what I wanted to do. I had too much energy and no direction: I was a member of the school swimming team, I organized the Friday afternoon tea dances, I studied hard at school and did well, but it wasn't enough. My mother had a lot of love and feeling, but no answers.

Then, by chance, a friend involved in dance invited me to go to a ballet studio to watch a class. I'd never seen a class, I'd never even seen a live ballet performance, since my native Canada at the time had almost no dance companies. But the quiet concentration of the dancers at the barre seemed so comfortable and right. I couldn't wait to get home to convince my mother to let me take class: I knew right away that this was something I wanted to try, that it was something I was going to like.

My adventure in self-discovery began with that chance encounter with ballet, and the adventure has never ceased. In reaching the end of one road—after enjoying the rewards given for hard work and dedication—I have always found another, sometimes unexpected path that has led me to yet more discoveries. Of course, I don't mean to make my first step sound easy. For one thing, the world was in the midst of the Depression, and money was limited. (In fact, just before I had to convince my family that I needed money so I could take class, I had been through the trauma of not being able to get the spring coat I had fallen in love with because it cost five dollars more than my mother had budgeted!) But perhaps because she saw in my determination to dance the right direction for my energies, my mother found a way to pay for three months of classes, one day a week.

I began to study with a wonderful teacher who was consistent and exact, who never confused me, who never made dance boring but always a challenge. Mr. Volkoff, a Russian émigré with marvelous training and impeccable taste, gave me the great beginnings that are so important to a dancer. He taught the body with precision, but he also taught his students to keep their minds open and flexible for all the possibilities of dance. He helped to prepare us for further discovery.

When that first series of classes came to an end, I had acquired such a longing to continue the experience that I found a way to go on—as a scholarship student, and after I finished school, by working at night to pay for classes and eventually to extend myself by going to New York.

The chance to discover yourself through dance—all kinds of dance, from classical ballet and modern to jazz and ethnic forms—is a privilege that comes to young people when they are fortunate enough to find what dance can give them. No one is ever going to force you to dance. There are not always little gifts for your efforts, it's not always uphill. Often there are dark moments when you're floundering. But the fact that you are doing something that requires effort and concen-

Rehearsing with *Amahl and the Night Visitors.*

tration, and are trying to express through movement the person you are, gives you the energy to continue. You learn to focus your intentions, to accept responsibility for yourself—both as the dancer and the *person* who is dancing. This is true, no matter what level you have reached in dance.

The discoveries never end, and the rewards are very special. Years after I began to study, I danced my first *Coppélia* as a guest with the National Ballet of Canada. Mr. Volkoff traveled from Toronto to be in the audience to see where his beginnings and mine had led me. His pride in seeing me perform was as great a reward for me as the applause of the audience.

The desire to dance isn't enough; you have to shape it and focus it and learn everything about yourself and your art that you can. You start with a good foundation, the best available, in whatever style of dance you have chosen, and you learn very early that there will always be something new to discover, about dance and about yourself. You never close your mind to what you may be able to do that you haven't yet done.

Every human being is born not only able, but eager to move. It's a basic instinct; we have a natural joy in movement. Dancers take the instinct and the desire to use their bodies for self-expression, and impose on them the discipline of dance training to create a perfect instrument that speaks in space and time. It is not an end accomplished overnight, but the journey from desire to fulfillment is, to my view, the most exciting experience a person can have.

When I began to study ballet, I had few points of comparison, no role models, no real choices. I fell in love with dance at first sight, but the future was clouded with doubts and insecurities. My family neither pushed nor held me back, but I was learning to dance at a time when a *life* in dance was about as uncertain as any I might choose. Today, I think, there should be no such feeling of doubt. Dance, in the decades since I began, has become a significant cultural force. Young people have so much marvelous exposure to what dance is— through regional ballet festivals, live performances of local and national companies, even television. They have so many choices that were denied dancers of my generation, simply because dance did not exist on the scale it does today.

Of course, answers are not simply handed out—you have to ask questions, listen, and learn. This is as much a part of becoming a dancer as learning "steps." Some things never change, among them the necessity of existing as a creative individual, a dancer, among nondancers who may be perplexed by your determination and desire.

"Can you really enjoy hours of learning movements and stretching muscles until they ache?" they will ask.

For the dancer, it's not a question; it is his or her life. There has to be a sense of achievement in the learning of dance technique, as much as in putting on a costume and makeup and performing for an audience. Nondancers can understand the applause; the mysteries of preparation are sometimes beyond them. Yet a good portion of the dancer's life consists of preparation to perform, and often it means giving up for a time some parts of life that others believe are important.

I had to make decisions about forgoing school social activities, dates, dances, and hanging around with friends because it was more important for me to go to dance class. No dedicated young dancer ever gets through his or her training without surrendering some of what people consider "pleasures," but the focus of dancing makes them seem trivial in comparison to the dream. Parents and friends are concerned that the young dancer is "missing" something, yet dancers have to make the effort to keep the lines of communication open with the important people in their lives, to help them accept if not understand, in the same way a dancer does, what the desire to dance means. Coming to terms with the nondancing world is just one more aspect of becoming a dancer.

Don't make the mistake, then, of assuming that the dance world is so unique in its drives and dreams that you are completely divorced from the rest of humanity. Don't ever forget that you are a *person who dances* as well as a dancer who happens to be a daughter or son, husband or wife, friend or lover.

It is true that to understand a dancer completely, you have to be a dancer. If you haven't done it, haven't felt it, you probably can't understand how a dancer feels about dance. But how he or she feels as a human being who happens to have chosen to express something through movement rather than through being a doctor or a writer or a lawyer or a teacher, what the triumphs and rejections, joys and self-doubts of life mean—these are matters that draw support and caring

Rehearsing with Mr. Balanchine and Herbert Bliss.

from those who love the dancer, whether or not they have the slightest notion of what dance is.

When I was performing with the New York City Ballet, a young dancer whom I had actually taught when she was a child and who was now a member of the company came to me in tears. She was dealing with aching problems: negative feelings about herself, a romantic crisis, a feeling of intimidation and rejection in the highly selective, competitive world of a major ballet company. She wanted me to help her, to give her reassurance and support.

I could understand her insecurity about her job, and could promise her that she wasn't likely to be fired, that all company members had moments of feeling passed over by the management and that this did not necessarily constitute a rejection of them as dancers.

"But why don't you talk to your mother?" I suggested.

"She won't understand, she's not a dancer."

"You don't have to be a dancer to know what it means to feel bad about yourself."

"No," she said stubbornly. "She's not a dancer, she can't understand me."

What a pity, I thought at the time, and continued to feel about this young woman throughout her career, that she had failed to create essential lines of communication with her family and those who should be closest to her because she had forgotten the person in her drive to be the dancer. Ironically, I believe she ultimately failed as the dancer for that very reason: Commitment to dance will not carry you through a lifetime without an equal commitment to being a whole person from which the artist draws inspiration and understanding in performance.

Never blame your problems as a person on the fact that you are a dancer. This is crippling, a weak excuse for not succeeding, when the fault, perhaps, lies in your own attitude toward dance and the world in which you must live.

You are the sum total of all your experiences, not just dance alone. Your image as a dancer is important; it defines you. Dance is your focus, but you can be anything besides, have many lives, if you want them badly enough. And what you want to express in dance that will move an audience to love and applaud you can be acquired only through constant awareness, education, sensitivity, and experience in the world outside of dance.

A couple of my advanced students, young women of eighteen or so, close to embarking on professional careers, asked me not long ago how I had managed to have a long career as a dancer onstage almost every night, to be married for a good many years, and to have had two children who are now grown up.

I answered without thinking: "It was good organization."

Never once in all that time did it occur to me that because I was a dancer, I was automatically cut off from any of life's experiences. The only problem was finding a way to do it all efficiently.

I believe that if you want to be a dancer strongly enough and it brings you complete enjoyment as it did me, you will be successful. Through the satisfactions of that success, you can afford to expand your life emotionally beyond dancing to encompass any kind of relationship, any type of existence that pleases you. If you want everything, if you take the responsibility for yourself and refuse to be diverted or stopped in your quest for your dream by the judgments of others, you can do it. And you will find a way to manage the organization.

When I first came to New York from Canada to see if I could work as a dancer, I had some seven years of ballet training behind me. I also had the determination to dance that had struck me the day I first set foot in Mr. Volkoff's studio. I believed that the combination was unbeatable.

Fortunately, I was able to find a job quickly, as a dancer in the corps de ballet of the Radio City Music Hall, so I could support myself and continue my dance studies. But I wanted to dance with a ballet company. Then an opportunity to audition for such a company arrived, and I went to it full of confidence. I was told that I was "too old."

I was about twenty-two at the time.

I didn't accept that label—or any other that was ever given me. I don't think any dancer ought to believe labels: too old, too short, too tall, too blond. It's a built-in way to defeat your desire to dance, another excuse to push off the responsibility for yourself onto the preconceived ideas of other people.

Ultimately, chance again played a part in the next step in my ca-

With Jacques d'Amboise in *The Nutcracker*.

reer. I was hired as a member of a major ballet company because a dancer my height was needed for *Swan Lake*. Within nine months from the time I started dancing with the company, I was a soloist. I was never "too old" again; I was judged by the only criterion that is valid: my ability as a dancer.

Talent and the Dancer

The dancer throughout his or her career is always testing ability, trying to grow as a performer and to express more perfectly the movements the choreography demands.

Some people talk about "talent," particularly people who are outside dance. "Talent" is viewed as a gift which, if one has it, will carry one through effortlessly. Talent is only the starting point for ability, and in the end it should not be a factor in the young person's efforts to become a dancer.

I cannot count the numbers of mothers who have come to me as a teacher to ask if their son or daughter has "talent." I suspect that what those parents are really asking is, "Are people going to love my child?" "Will he or she actually earn a living doing this, and be happy?" (People do not, on the other hand, question whether the student in, say, medical school is going to be happy as a doctor or whether the future doctor has any "talent" for medicine, so presumably the major focus in these parents' questions truly is the economics of the dancer's life.)

Some of these parents are also begging to be told that their child is more than "talented"—that he or she is a genius.

Geniuses, alas, are few. Supremely talented dancers—the Baryshnikovs, Nureyevs, and Fonteyns—are rare individuals. There are not many Einsteins or Michelangelos or Mozarts either. It is fruitless for you or your parents to worry about whether you are one of them. If you are, you know it, just as if you have what the world calls talent, you will prove it in the execution of your art. Neither talent nor genius is a question for student or parents. What is important is the desire and the determination and the willingness to apply discipline to them to shape ability.

The only "talent" I acknowledge in the student is the talent for learning, for hearing what I am saying as the teacher, instead of simply listening. I can judge that a student has physical ability, good coordination, muscles capable of acquiring memories of movement that can be reproduced, without conscious thought, perfectly every time. I can see in students a sense of responsibility and application, an awareness of a strong self-image as a dancer. I can sense intention and dedication. I do not know if these matters are what parents think of as "talent," but I do know that the desire to dance will remain forever unfulfilled if the dancer lacks them. Without them, there is no "talent."

For the student, there is only one end, and that is to dance. Talent is a label like any other, and it can be as defeating as any other, however positive its connotations. It is far too easy to fall back on "talent," if the label has been applied to the dancer, as an excuse for not making the effort to acquire the discipline and develop the *ability to dance.*

The body is the instrument and the steps of dance are the tools. Together they produce movement, and when the audience perceives the movement as a series of beautiful pictures in space, the student has begun to dance. When those pictures become a visual portrayal of the accompanying music, then the student is a dancer.

This is the beginning and the end of the desire to dance. The responsibility and the discovery belong to the dancer. I hope that I can contribute to the discovery, as a dancer speaking to dancers who are at the beginning of a road that I chose without hesitation because of the accidental encounter with a ballet class.

I have lived with dance for most of my life, and I couldn't live without it. I wish I could give back to dance all that I have gained from it. What I can give back to young dancers are not only facts and knowledge about dance and being a dancer, but also the reassurance to those of you who are in the process of learning that the joy doesn't fade, that the discoveries you make about your art and yourself are always exciting, and that anyone who is willing to shape the desire to dance with work and discipline is going to find an arena in which to perform—a way to be a dancer.

2

LEARNING TO DANCE

In no place in the world at this time do people dance as much as they do in the United States. Social, theatrical, traditional, dance is and has always been a deeply ingrained form of expression, drawing its impulses from hundreds of cultural and artistic sources and integrating them into a broad concept of American dance.

Native American Indians danced before the first Europeans landed; settlers from distant lands brought traditional folk dances and kept them alive; slaves from Africa carried with them often nothing but the rhythms and movements of the cultures they were separated from. Dance as a social event has existed in America from the days of frontier square dances to nights in glittering discos.

And what, you may ask, has this tradition of popular dance to do with the desire to dance on a stage before an audience as a classical ballet dancer or modern dancer? Only this, and I think it is an aspect of dance that makes it such a unique and vital cultural tradition in

America: When classical ballet made its way to these shores from the courts of Europe, followed some years later by forms of modern dance, it was rapidly assimilated by a nation accustomed to dance, was reshaped by the genius of American choreographers who drew on all available resources and added to the vocabulary of formal dance, and was then exported again around the world.

Dance in America is not an art for a cultural elite, but an integral part of our heritage. Any young dancer ought to appreciate that whatever his or her chosen discipline, one is never set apart, but is firmly attached to a broad and enduring world of dance. Such knowledge is essential: you must be open to experiences and possibilities if you want to succeed. I have found my particular joy in classical ballet; another may find it in the disciplines of modern or jazz dance; still others may achieve their satisfactions in theatrical forms of ethnic dance. But we are all brothers and sisters in the world of dance. We share a desire to dance and we exchange techniques and vocabulary for the greater expression of our art, looking back always to a strong stream of dance on the popular level.

The real distinction we have to make as disciplined dancers is between the popular and the theatrical experiences. Everything contributes to dance in America, and the most uniquely American discovery in dance has been how the formal disciplines and the popular forms can be melded into dance for the musical theater. Mexican, African, Cuban, Spanish styles of dance have been integrated into the musical theater; classical ballet has been combined with modern techniques and utilized theatrically; jazz dance and classical ballet have been successfully joined. Performers, teachers, and choreographers raised in the traditions of Russian ballet came to this country in the wake of the Russian Revolution and established a new tradition; France, England, Denmark, and Holland have also fed classical ballet with their traditions. Modern dance in its theatrical form came from Germany, and grew with the efforts of Isadora Duncan, Ruth St. Denis, Ted Shawn, Martha Graham, and Hanya Holm.

No dancer today is limited in choosing the form of dance he or she feels best serves the creative impulse. We have in America schools and styles of dance to encompass every permutation, from classical ballet to the techniques of modern dance to forms that draw on ethnic sources.

If you have the desire to dance and the willingness to submit yourself to a discipline through which to work toward that perfect instrument—the body that can dance—no place in the world will you find so many opportunities and so many excellent teachers as in the United States today. And at no time in the history of dance in America has there been such enthusiasm and acceptance of theatrical dance—it is a renaissance that is reaching every level of society, opening up possibilities for dance, and drawing young dancers from all parts of the country.

What Kind of Training Is "Best"?

The "best" in any kind of creative activity can be defined in only one way: a good teacher teaching a dedicated student; a good teacher who encourages discovery teaching a student who is open to new experiences.

Beyond this, it is very much the responsibility of the dancer to decide what form of dance he or she wishes as the primary discipline. The discovery of what is available is part of becoming a dancer. You are guided by your tastes and the kinds of feelings you have about yourself, which will be formed into the image of yourself as dancer.

My dance allegiance as a performer is, of course, to ballet, yet I would not recommend any style of training or any form of dance over another. I do believe, though, that *correct early training* is the best kind of training, regardless of syllabus or methodology. In ballet, whether the training is based on the Cecchetti method, or Bournonville, Vaganova, or Royal Academy of Dance, it should be properly taught. At the very beginning of training, the first two or three years, what matters is that you learn the correct muscle memory; if you have been taught incorrectly, it is difficult in later years to erase the muscle memory and retrain the body. This can take time, and mean a tremendous emotional toll and even bodily harm.

Muscle memory—what is it really? Muscle memory is the involuntary reaction of muscles to the practice of a movement. The body will practice a movement or a step, which is one word in the vocabulary of dance—a *plié*, for example. The dancer practices the movement in a very exact way, over and over again without a mistake, and the muscles remember. Ideally, once the muscles have learned the movement, they will do it in exactly the same form and will execute it without conscious thought. These are the memories the beginning dancer learns, whether he or she starts at eight, or fifteen, or twenty, whether the style of dance is classical ballet, Spanish dancing, modern dance, or tap dancing.

Good training is a valid syllabus that brings rapid progress in learning the vocabulary, so that within two, three, or five years, depending on the dancer's age (the older dancer often has more accelerated progress because the body structure is not changing as much as in a younger person), he or she has a total command of the vocabulary, and knows the words and some phrases. The dancer is ready for the connections between isolated movements—ready to make sentences and paragraphs in dance.

It is at this point that being wedded to a syllabus is often not particularly good. I am not criticizing any specific syllabus of dance, only the idea that a rigidly structured system concentrates so much upon the words—the individual movements—that the sentences, and the challenge they present to the dancer, are overlooked. If you don't have a challenge for the muscle memory you have expended so much emotional and physical energy on developing, if you keep practicing only the same words, the same phrases, never going beyond what is in the book, muscle boredom will set in. Instead of making you better, all that practice simply becomes a waste of energy.

The inventive teacher will go beyond the system, will be aware of time and space, as well as vocabulary, will show the student how to speak in sentences, will teach him or her not just steps but *enchaînement,* the combination of steps that makes a creative statement in space and time. This is true of all styles of dance.

Similarly, for all styles of dance, to get the best training there must be a chemistry between teacher and student, and a respect between the two for what each is doing. There can be no holding back. If you lack the emotional rapport with your teacher that is essential to the worlds of discovery in dance, I don't believe you can learn.

Although the styles of dance syllabuses—how you move in space, the movement and placement of arms, head, legs, and torso—can be quite regimented, creative dance is not at all regimented; it is a con-

Dance is movement.

stant search for artistic expression. I offer, though, the following reminders about dance training, when you are looking for the "best":

1. When you begin training, complete one syllabus, but be aware of muscle boredom.

2. No system can give your body a full discovery of its potential; all it can give you is the correct vocabulary.

3. Training creates muscle memory that becomes involuntary. With it, you are designing your body as an instrument to be used by a choreographer—or yourself as choreographer.

4. Statements of movements, phrases in time and space, not just steps but *enchaînement*—this is what good training gives you, once you have mastered the vocabulary.

5. The more systems and forms of dance you experience, the clearer and more far-reaching your focus will be; this is the aim of your training. But you must begin within the limits of a single system and then grow beyond it, keeping your mind and body open to discovery as you reach for perfection.

Classical Dance/Modern Dance

Young dancers in America have the opportunity to dance in an enormous variety of fields. But the dance world is competitive; there have probably never been so many dedicated and talented young dancers. As one of my students remarked, "It can be a terrible feeling to walk into an audition with a hundred other dancers, all wanting that one available job, and you know they've all studied just as hard as you have."

A dancer today has to be prepared to work when the chance comes, whatever the demands of the job. For example, musical comedy today is no longer tap-dancing chorus boys and girls, but a showcase for dance that combines elements of ballet and modern dance, jazz dance, ethnic dance, and all forms of theatrical dance, depending on the vision of the choreographer (and many Broadway and movie choreographers come from ballet, modern, and ethnic backgrounds). If you want a career in dance, you have to be *dancing*. It doesn't necessarily have to be with a major ballet company or an important modern company. The theatrical experience, dancing before an audience (and not an audience of one) is what is important, and the wider your range of technical abilities, whatever your primary discipline, the better off you will be when it comes to finding your place in dance.

The vocabularies of modern and classical dance are different, and the discovery of comfort in the discipline you choose as your primary one depends, perhaps, on personality. In classical dance, you learn the structure in order to create a particular kind of picture in space and in time. The limits of the discipline are well defined, and the dancer uses the limits for self-expression. It is somewhat like writing poetry in a strict sonnet form, and classical ballet dancers find that the form answers a need in themselves. I, for one, felt totally comfortable on *pointe* as soon as I wore toe shoes. Even now, when I am not performing but teaching, I prefer pointe shoes. And I am satisfied by the technical limits of ballet and its boundless opportunities for expression.

Modern dance is freer in expression and technique, more like using a learned vocabulary to write free verse. One of the best expressions of the nature of modern dance comes from Jerry Bywaters Cochran, dancer, teacher, and choreographer, who is the director of an outstanding school of modern dance in Dallas, Texas: "Modern dance is both a technique and a point of view. The technique had its beginnings in the 1920s in reaction to the theater dance practiced at that time, and in a search for an earlier, more natural form of movement. The early pioneers were Isadora Duncan, Ruth St. Denis, and Ted Shawn.

"The modern dancers who followed tended to leave their own personal variants on the technique, and as a result we often hear modern dance referred to as a number of techniques, with those of Graham, Humphrey-Weidman, Holm-Wigman, Horton, Limón, Louis-Nikolais, Lewitzky, and Cunningham being the most significant.

"Even so, the various techniques have much in common. All use both the flexed and pointed foot, the turned out and parallel positions of the body. All have explored the dancer's relationship to the floor as in controlled falls into the floor and movement seated on the floor. And all have tried to integrate the entire body into movement—the torso as well as the extremities.

"Almost more important is modern dance as a point of view. From the beginning modern dancers have emphasized the importance of dance as communication, not display; and such qualities of individuality, experimentation, and improvisation over adherence to a fixed and rigid system of movement."

To my mind, in spite of the differences in the two forms, any dancer who chooses one or the other as the primary discipline will encounter no conflict if he or she chooses to study the other as a second discipline. This is not to say that a beginning dancer who is in the process of learning the vocabulary of either form should attempt both at the same time. Focus is terribly important for a young dancer; muscles have to be taught a memory by constant practice until their movement is involuntary. But once the initial stages are passed, it is not necessary to spend several years of study in one form before undertaking to learn another, provided you study with a good teacher.

For example, a modern dancer will come to my beginning pointe class not to become a classical dancer, but because she has discovered that by doing the exercises on pointe, she will develop strength in her ankles, improve their flexibility, and actually discover a new center of her body. Classical dance training concentrates on placement, including the extremities (feet, legs, arms, head), while modern dance gives the dancer more of a feeling of the torso. The classical ballet dancer can profit from the modern techniques that develop a strong back and great strength in the back of the legs.

An intelligent dancer can only benefit by combining the two dance disciplines, especially in today's dance world, where the boundaries between the two forms are gradually blurring. While we will always have distinct definitions of classical dance and modern dance, we are also experiencing a phenomenon called "contemporary dance" that demands techniques from dancers that Tchaikovsky never dreamed of when he composed *Swan Lake*.

George Balanchine is a perfect example of a contemporary choreographer who uses dance that refers visually to what modern dance means to him, but who is firmly based in classical technique. The dancers in his ballets look wonderful doing the movements he creates from this fusion of styles. The same dancers look equally wonderful in such classical ballets as *Sleeping Beauty*.

I can't emphasize enough the importance of being open to all kinds of discoveries in dance and being prepared to dance whatever is

Ask, listen, and look.

required by the choreographer. Balanchine and Martha Graham, to take one example, collaborated on the ballet *Episodes* to the music of Webern. The first half of the program was based on her choreography and was danced by her company and one member of the ballet company. The second half was Balanchine's choreography, but in addition, he designed movement on a modern dancer, Paul Taylor (then a member of Martha Graham's company), using his impression of Taylor's body to create new movement, a marvelous marriage of dance styles.

Balanchine's jazz ballet, *Modern Jazz: Variants*, had the Modern Jazz Quartet onstage, an orchestra in the pit, and two couples dancing —three of them classically trained and the fourth a jazz/modern dancer—to express his concept of what jazz movement was. Another Balanchine ballet, *Square Dance*, with a caller onstage, used the form of square dancing done in the classical idiom.

I believe, then, that a classical ballet dancer who is aiming for a professional career, and who has received good training in ballet technique, can expand his or her capabilities by studying modern dance. A couple of years of study of classical dance cannot help but give the modern dancer a new approach to movement. Although I see my students making the effort to study with modern teachers, and have experienced modern dancers in my classical ballet classes, the most impressive revelation of the value of study in both forms has come to me through my years of developing college dance programs and traveling around the country seeing dance programs in high schools of performing arts and other dance centers. I have seen how much the study of both classical and modern dance has given to young dancers in terms of development and experience.

The infinite possibilities for discovery of what the body can do, what it can express, the forms that creativity can take, should never be dismissed because the dancer has defined himself or herself solely in terms of the primary discipline.

Opportunities and Conflicts

In general terms, it is probably easier for the beginning dancer to find a school of ballet than it is to find a good studio that teaches modern dance. Centers of modern dance are concentrated pretty much on the two coasts and in some large cities in between. Young children are often exposed to "creative movement" in the public school system, but usually the teen-age years bring young people the opportunity and desire to study dance. Ballet is frequently one of the most available forms, but there may be several others to choose from. Yet, I urge young dancers not to spread themselves too thin at the beginning. There are dance schools that offer tap, toe, acrobatic, baton twirling, and jazz dance within an hour or two a couple of times a week. The social value of such schools for the teenager who wants to experience movement in its different forms is not to be negated. However, although the young dancer has not lost anything by experiencing basic ballet in such schools, it is not, I think, possible to develop a real concentration if the program is too varied. The desire to dance has to be focused and disciplined.

Choose one discipline or another as your first discipline, until you feel strong in it so that you can go on to support yourself in another. Then you are capable of deciding whether to stay with the primary discipline or move wholeheartedly into another. Sometimes trained classical dancers will discover they feel more comfortable in modern dance, because the feet aren't working well, there are problems with pointe, the ankles are stiff. They frequently discover they have more freedom and joy in moving by turning to modern dance. I know many classically trained dancers who have studied for as long as eight or ten years and have found that jazz or modern dance is more to their liking —and many of them later come back to classical ballet because what the other forms have given them have made them more capable and intelligent dancers.

The point is that you must love the discipline and you must have a basis of trust in your body, a vocabulary, a basic training—and the knowledge that this alone won't satisfy you. The instrument you are developing must be constantly open to new experiences. It is up to you to find them, either in study or in performances that stretch your technique.

Although I have concentrated on the interdisciplinary questions of classical and modern dance, what I say applies as readily to the dancer who develops his or her technique at the community center level in, for example, forms of ethnic dance. The disciplined expression of an art that has its roots in one of the many cultures that make up the nation is as valid a dance form as the ballets of Mr. Balanchine or Martha Graham. The dancer who has the opportunity and the focus to perfect the techniques taught in such centers is prepared to expand his or her abilities in any direction.

The more you put into your body, the more discoveries you make, the more muscle memory, the more experience, the more developed your senses, the greater are your horizons for self-expression in dance.

For the study of any dance discipline, a good teacher is important. For modern dance, it should be mentioned that there are fewer modern dance teachers who have studied with one or another of the significant figures in the field than is the case with classical ballet, which has a longer and more widespread tradition. The matter is complicated by the fact that the great exponents of modern dance do not work within a system of rules and regulations as classical ballet does, but have rather danced and had an impact on the basis of very personal visions. It is not easy for a teacher to share such a vision with students. On the other hand, the experience of such study can be instrumental in triggering the student's own vision, if the chemistry between teacher and student exists.

It is important in undertaking the study of modern dance, either as a beginner or as a classical dancer seeking new experiences, to study with the very best teachers. Martha Graham and others of her stature in the field of modern dance have expressed hope that some form of systemized training can be developed so that the terminology and description of modern dance movement will be more accessible to students and teachers.

A knowledge of both ballet and modern dance can be advantageous in terms of careers. The vocabulary of each enhances the other; each form, modern and classical ballet, gives new and different strengths to various parts of the body. But is there any conflict?

The only conflict I have ever noticed between different disciplines of dance (and I speak particularly of classical and modern) is a mental one. On the one hand, one can encounter teachers who do not see any reason to encourage dual study. They are the kind who say, "Don't listen to anyone but me; don't learn anything that I don't teach you." Yet the truth is, there is so much to be discovered in dance—no single person has all the answers. The dancer takes from the teacher as much as the teacher has to give, but there is always someone over the horizon who can give something more, something different, a new experience or new strengths. Good teachers, whatever their principal area of interest, can only complement each other.

On the other hand, the conflict may exist in the dancer's mind, in the belief that it is impossible to meld two forms of dance to the dancer's advantage. If the dancer fails to become aware of how two forms of dance can complement each other, he or she is setting up conditions that may eventually mean muscle conflict. Most important, the reluctance to leave oneself open to discovery—which is what dance ought to be every day of the dancer's life—may mean missing the opportunity to participate in a professional experience with a dance company, whether in a large city or a small town. Artistic directors of dance companies seek dancers who can perform the choreography; they are not looking for dancers who can't because they've never taken the opportunity to learn.

Be open to all performing experiences—I'd like all dancers to remind themselves of that every day of their lives. The dancer's body is a physical instrument through which choreographers—from those of the New York City Ballet and American Ballet Theatre to Paul Taylor, Twyla Tharp, and Alvin Ailey (to name only three of many) —express their creative ideas. But the dancer must also practice a mental attitude that leaves the mind open to accept whatever the world of dance has to offer.

PART II
Studying Dance

3

TEACHERS
AND TRAINING

You can't learn to dance by reading a book on how it's done; you can't
practice dancing at home alone; you can't see yourself change and
develop in a room lined with mirrors. Not even with videotape can
you sit in judgment on yourself as a dancer and be objective. In part,
it is the young dancer's lack of experience that makes self-teaching
and self-criticism practical impossibilities; in part, it is that no reflection—mirrors, television, tape—conveys the same impact as the three-
dimensional dancer moving in space and time. Another eye that
stands in for the audience and views the dancer with both experience
and objectivity is necessary. This is true whether you have been studying dance for years or are just beginning.

The other eye, of course, belongs to the teacher.

Since I have become a teacher myself, after years of studying with
excellent and inspiring people, both men and women, I have been
able to combine the two perspectives, and can offer some considerations about what constitutes good teaching.

I have had inspiring teachers, but the truth is, their "inspiration" had less to do with their emotional outflow than their ability to allow me to discover the inspiration within me. As I said earlier, there was that chemistry between teacher and student, and trust. But teaching means *to teach*; it doesn't mean to accept. Too many young people go to teachers who are accepting of the students, who then begin to feel very comfortable. Such teachers merely polish that comfort; there is no discovery in what they "teach."

A good teacher will let you see beyond the hard work to what you can become; he or she will make you want to become whatever you are capable of, because you are discovering dance through proper teaching.

What is "proper" teaching?

Ballet, to take the form I know best, is logical and scientific; the rules of classical dance don't harm you, but incorrect teaching can. You can learn the wrong kinds of muscle memory, if the teacher cannot see or doesn't know how to express what you're doing improperly. A good teacher not only knows how to teach a young dancer the vocabulary of ballet and the structure of classical dance, but is also aware of the rhythms of movement and the lines of the body, so that each movement has a clean shape to it.

It is absolutely necessary for both student and teacher to understand that the dance vocabulary has a rhythm to it—a timing based on the music and related to the very exact steps that are the fundamentals of dance. This is especially true of classical dance, which can easily fall into a mechanical repetition of steps if the concept of time (that is, the rhythm of the music) is not intimately joined to the movement in space. It is equally true of modern and other forms of contemporary dance; it is true even of such specialized forms as stylized Far Eastern dance (Balinese, Thai, Indian), where the formal "poses" are actually constant movement related to the timing of the accompaniment.

A good teacher has to be not only capable of honest, exact teaching that still leaves the dancer open to new discoveries, but also willing to answer questions: about training, about the physical and emotional problems a student encounters, and the experiences he or she will undergo as a dancer. Why does this muscle hurt? Why do I have trouble jumping? What caused my tendonitis?

The teacher of dance has an enormous responsibility. So much of what the dancer's future will be rests with him or her, since the only frame of reference in terms of progress and execution for the student is the teacher and the class. Dance is an emotional and intellectual experience for both observer and performer. The teacher has to do more than teach the structure of a movement. He or she has to teach a way of putting the structure in a context that expresses its emotional content and its flow.

Choosing a Teacher

Teaching dance is highly individual, however structured the form of the dance itself. It wouldn't be fair of me to give absolute qualities for any teacher—except for the chemistry and the honesty I have already mentioned.

The only real basis for judging a teacher is the product he or she turns out: good dancers. This means that the classes provide focus, and are not designed as a form of entertainment for the student who wants to experience a smattering of the possibilities of movement.

Teachers who have had the opportunity to perform have, as a general rule, a greater knowledge to impart, since they have experienced the choreography of others and the fact of exposing themselves and their abilities onstage in front of an audience. Yet I know of superb teachers who have never had a performing career. Their professional training is such that it enables them to give students the sense of the musicality of movement.

On a local basis, a teacher who participates in the dance life of the community—encouraging performances, heading a local dance company, providing dance demonstrations for the school system and elsewhere—has a valuable attitude about dance, and will convey it to students. And the teacher whose students do well in the wider dance world beyond the classroom is one who encourages discovery. For example, have his or her students gone on from the local setting to study in the much more competitive arena of New York or some other major dance center? Have some, at least, become professionals? Do students participate in regional dance festivals sponsored by the National Asso-

Communication.

Response.

Belief.

ciation for Regional Ballet; do they compare well with the students of other teachers in the region? (Chapter 11 deals with the regional dance movement and its activities.)

These are the only broad judgments that can be made about the quality of a teacher of dance. A great deal depends on the student's perceptions, and his or her willingness to learn how to judge. Your progress and the progress of the other students in the class serve as a guide, along with gaining a basis of comparison with other teachers, other dancers.

Go to see dance, whether it is a performance at a college or university given by a dance group associated with the institution, a touring group (the National Endowment for the Arts sponsors several locally and nationally), community dance groups in performance, or performances at regional dance festivals. And now television provides another opportunity. While the problems of televising ballet and other forms of dance have yet to be overcome (and may never be—a picture of dance can't make you cry the way recorded music can), recent efforts to preserve ballet performances via videotape have made available to the whole country the chance to catch a glimpse of classical dance. You will learn a lot from live and televised performances about what you should eventually be able to do, what the teaching you are receiving ought to be leading you to.

With the spread of interest in all kinds of theatrical dance, many areas that were once out of the mainstream of dance are now becoming dance centers. The regional ballet movement has had an enormous impact on the dance life of this country. With increasing frequency, guest teachers from New York and other large cities are invited to all five regions (Southeast, Southwest, Pacific, Northeast, Mid-States; see also Appendix) to hold master classes for a day or two; there are chances at regional festivals to take class with a distinguished teacher. Modern dance classes at community centers enable students to experience teaching different from their usual classes. The point is to make the effort to discover a basis of comparison between what you are learning and what others teach.

With regard to teachers, there is one further point that must be emphasized. It is the matter of comfort, which will come up again and again in these pages and in the dancer's life.

"Comfort" has two meanings for the dancer, one good and one not so good. If "comfort" means that the chemistry between student and teacher is working, and the challenge of new discoveries is "comfortable" and satisfying, this is good. If you are at ease in the environment, in a studio, in a class, this is a positive kind of comfort. I can't define it any better than to say that one place feels right to you, while another doesn't.

The comfort I felt when I first walked into Mr. Volkoff's studio before I ever began to study dance gave me the sense of being in the right place with the right person. The next two years with this teacher challenged me, kept my interest engaged, nourished my desire to dance. That was true comfort.

Now, what about "bad" comfort? Teaching that doesn't do more than re-create familiar steps and exercises and movements may be "comfortable"—easy on the student, who doesn't have to be bothered with challenges to do more and better—but it's the wrong kind of comfort. A teacher who accepts this and doesn't require students to extend themselves daily to make new discoveries about dance is not going to prepare them to learn understanding as well as steps. And beyond the steps are the combinations, and farther along the road is the stiff competition the dancer is going to meet when he or she wants to perform. There is so much to be learned, and ease and comfort will not teach much.

It is the dancer's responsibility to demand to be challenged.

After I had been dancing for some years with the New York City Ballet, I was asked by Mr. Balanchine to perform again a role I had created in the ballet's initial performance a number of years before. I was aware that Mr. Balanchine was watching my performance from the wings, as I re-created the choreography he had first designed for a younger and less experienced dancer. When I came offstage, he was clearly pleased with the performance, but his comment seems to me to carry the essence of what learning to dance is all about—what the teacher teaches and the dancer learns in the pursuit of the perfect instrument.

He said only: "A young dancer dances the steps; an experienced dancer dances the movements—with understanding."

A teacher can teach you the steps. That will set you free to take what you have learned to dance the movements with understanding and make pictures in space—and that is what real dancing is. It is done with joy.

Out in the World: Further Dance Training

The young dancer in smaller cities and towns has a limited opportunity to test his or her abilities against other dancers. Of course, it can be highly gratifying to be a "star" in your own hometown, to be the best student in your dance class, a featured performer in local productions or recitals. But even if you have no serious ambitions for a career in dance, you can't know what you are capable of until you can measure yourself against other standards. And by doing so, you will be giving yourself another experience of awareness.

Fortunately, in the past couple of decades, the regional ballet movement has gained both momentum and stature. Regional dance festivals give young dancers the chance to see and dance with the best dancers in their area, and to learn from one another—not only in terms of technique, but also in terms of emotional learning. The new perspective on your technique and abilities is essential. Although it may occasionally be discouraging to find that your best is not equal to that of other dancers you encounter, it can also be a source of encouragement to discover that your six or seven years of dance training have given you capabilities that do match those of the best dancers in your region.

The young modern dancer does not have the same regional organizations that are available to classical ballet dancers, although many contemporary and ethnic groups are associated with NARB. Yet the opportunities for comparison are there if you seek them out. It is worth the bus or train trip to a nearby city to take advantage of the modern classes so many community centers now offer. The many colleges that offer dance majors combine both ballet and modern, and the interested student can, even if he or she is not going to college, investigate the modern dance performances nearby colleges give and even, on an individual basis, participate in or observe actual classes.

The discipline of dance gives a core of strength that serves the dancer well through a lifetime. But strength untested is no strength at all. Ability that is not perfected is wasted in the long run. The serious young dancer has to take one further step in the testing and training process if he or she has any plans to use the years of basic training of the physical instrument for some artistic end. I believe this is true whether the goal is a professional career with a ballet or modern dance company, a career in the musical theater, as a teacher, as an occasional performer in the community, or a different kind of self-discovery—that a life as a dancer is not what he or she wants.

There is nothing wrong, I should add, with the latter decision. I have seen young dancers who have made the step from their hometowns to, for example, one of the excellent high schools of performing arts around the country for a period of intensive study. Instead of making the next logical step, which is study at a major ballet center with a view to becoming a professional or going to college to continue dance studies along with academic subjects, they have decided there is something else they want to experience. They have practiced a focus on dance; they feel they have completed the experience; and they are prepared to make a similar, focused commitment to a different life and different experiences. They have not lost by their years of dance training; they have achieved self-discovery and a focus that can be applied to any undertaking they choose.

For those who choose to continue to dance, the logical, and indeed essential, step is to go out into the world, seek further training where the standards are high, and take the responsibility for a commitment to advanced work.

This generally means going to New York or San Francisco, or possibly one of the other major dance centers across the country. I wish I could say that it doesn't matter—but, in a sense, it does. One of my students remarked: "New York is where it's at, we were always told that, we believed it, and now that I'm here, I know it's true."

It is true that overall, the best teachers, the best performances, the most teachers, and the most opportunities to experience the excellence of American dance are crammed into New York City. Coming to New York is in itself an intensive training for responsibility, for growing up and taking charge of your life, for learning how to survive in a new environment away from the comforts of home, for meeting people who will help you learn, help you get a job, help you find out more about yourself. Excellent teachers and performances exist all across the United States, and the student open to learning cannot help but profit from whatever the circumstances provide. But the truth is, there is no place like New York. I will suggest some alternatives to New York, but if you are a serious young dancer, it is a New York studio that you will be aiming for, and a perceptive local teacher should understand that this experience is something an able dancer needs.

Study in New York

People who come to New York to study dance always have a dream and an image of themselves as dancers. Otherwise they wouldn't uproot themselves from the comforts of home and friends to face difficult challenges. In a later chapter, we'll talk about some of the problems and perils of living as a young dancer in a strange city, but the first consideration has to be discovering where to study and what you must expect to learn, how you can get the most from the experience.

A young dancer may be able to spend only a few months in the city, especially if money is limited. Some dancers may get a great deal from a few months of studying in New York. For others, even a year isn't long enough; and some dancers may need two or three years. Although many dancers come to my studio for the summer and then return home to study during the rest of the year (often with a plan to return on a more extended basis when circumstances, such as school, permit), I think you must allow yourself six months to a year to get the most out of a teacher. If you are able to spend only two or three months in the city, you have to be ready to commit yourself to a stringent routine of study, but it is difficult to know whether you are improving greatly in such a short period.

One student who studied with me specified that she only had a year; if she wasn't prepared to audition successfully in that time, she had alternative goals for herself. We worked out a schedule for her that included studying modern dance as well. At my studio, she took ballet class, partnering, pointe work, and variations, with three modern classes a week at another studio. After a year, she had improved so that even though she had never auditioned before, she had such an image of herself as dancer and such confidence in her ability, she was able to walk into an audition with two hundred other dancers and be accepted as an apprentice with a major company. She was an able dancer, to be sure, but it was her commitment and focus, her work with someone she believed could help her, the right and "comfortable" environment of the studio that was in large part responsible for her success.

However talented and dedicated a young dancer is, I don't believe he or she should consider coming to a city like New York without close supervision until about the age of sixteen or seventeen. Institutional schools (which I will talk about later) do accept much younger students, but they are not left totally on their own and the schools take responsibility for them. The older student must understand that he or she is going to be asked to grow up very fast in a short period and take a great deal of responsibility for both study and living. If you don't have the initial maturity to handle such an intensive experience, you would do well to wait for a year or two.

The question of where you will study is a major one. The commitment in time and energy has to be worthwhile, and the financial considerations too are not minor. Although the period of study is equivalent to college or graduate study compressed into a comparatively short period, many parents balk at supporting a student dancer in New York for a year or two. Yet how much do four years of college cost? In comparison, the training of a dancer in New York is something of a bargain!

Some dancers do come to the city without the slightest idea of where they will study, but such cases are, I think, rare, and certainly should be. Many excellent teachers around the country are retired professional dancers or have trained with an established institutional school. They have an idea of the kind of teaching an advanced student will get from a particular teacher in New York—the dance world is not large, and reputations are well known. Very often, for example, the students who come to my studio from other places have been referred by teachers who were my professional colleagues or who share a similar philosophy of dance and training. They know that one of their students coming to New York to study with me will have a learning experience with the same artistic concept and direction as that from which they came. This sense of continuity contributes to the comfort they will find in their new situation, and makes easier the transition from hometown to strange new city, from a local class to classes made up of very good young dancers from all across the country.

Your teacher, with his or her knowledge of the dance experience, should be the first source of information. You may also encounter students who have trained for a time in New York and have returned to their hometowns. They can offer opinions and feelings about the studios at which they have studied. You can talk to dancers at regional dance festivals. You can write to New York studios for information about their classes. The major dance magazines, such as *Dance News* and *Dance Magazine*, contain valuable information about studios. The directors of important studios are frequently well-known figures in the dance world. You can readily find out what they have achieved professionally as dancers and teachers, what companies they have danced with, who their students have been. What is important is doing some preliminary research into the kinds of classes available, who the teachers are (most studios have more than one), what the cost of classes is. Remember that you have to live as well as study—and with intensive study, you will be using up shoes at a great rate, a major expense for the dancer.

Most studios have open classes, and you are free to come and go and take as many classes as you wish at whatever level you are capable of. You do, however, have to give the teacher a chance—several months, really—to teach you and help you improve. Studio hopping—trying one studio for a week or two, then another and another throughout your whole stay—is not productive. If you come to the city cold, without knowing where you're going, it's a good idea to allow yourself a week or two to go from one recommended school to another, take class, feel what the school is like, what your response to the teacher is. But don't be fooled by the fact that there are other young people your age there who seem to be happy. The way to examine a studio is to experience it physically.

Then you simply have to make a decision, and stick to it long enough (more than just a few classes) to discover whether there is something of value you can get from this studio you couldn't get anyplace else. Some students come to class for a few days, become quickly dissatisfied because it is too strange or too difficult or too challenging or not challenging enough, and go off to try another studio, only to return after a few weeks of studio hopping to start the process all over again.

There is, to be sure, a kind of adjustment that one makes to the environment of a school. Some schools are highly clinical in their approach, and a newcomer might find the atmosphere cool. Others are very friendly—but friendliness alone is not a criterion if it is not combined with effective teaching.

If you find that you are deeply unhappy with your situation after a number of weeks at a studio, it might be worth considering a change, but *only* after you have asked yourself some serious questions about *why* you are unhappy. Have you spent enough time to understand the teacher's approach? Are you unhappy because you feel that the teacher doesn't "like" you (and I've heard any number of students say this)? Do you feel you haven't been corrected enough or even that the teacher hasn't noticed you?

Is it true that the teacher isn't correcting you individually but is giving corrections to the class that you should be responding to? Do you respect the corrections that are made, trust the teacher, and respond in the proper way? If you are confused, do you ask the teacher, or just continue in confusion, thus not learning what you should?

What do you mean when you say the teacher doesn't like you? If you really feel that chemistry is totally lacking between you and the teacher, if he or she is not turned on by your efforts or you by the teacher's, you may have reached an impasse. A good teacher understands that a body dancing isn't like making a machine work by pushing buttons. But if there is intention, he or she will recognize it in the dancer. Are you trying? If you admit to yourself that you are not, then perhaps the teacher has good reason not to respond fully to you.

It is not all a question of liking and being liked, either. Even if you don't "like" the teacher, ask yourself if there is something you can get from that teacher that you couldn't get anywhere else. With the right attitude about what you can get from a teacher, you can't wholly dislike him or her, even if there is no question of being sentimentally attached.

There does come a time when a student leaves a teacher, and that time is something only the individual dancer recognizes. I worked with a teacher until I outgrew her, and then went on to the next, and the next. Once, early in my experience, after I had moved on, I tried going back to a teacher who had given me a great deal. I was bored. I had grown beyond what she was able to teach, excellent though she was for me at a certain point in my discovery of dance.

A good student *takes* from a teacher, until that teacher has been drained dry, and then he or she goes on to fresh discoveries. This is your responsibility, and this is why I believe that studying in New York demands that the dancer take the time to *take*—to absorb and digest, and not to skim, to make changes not on the basis of emotional

Listen to corrections—don't be too comfortable.

reactions, but as the result of self-knowledge and self-examination. The student who is contemplating a move to New York for further study has several years of training behind him or her; the fundamentals have been learned. But he or she ought to have as well the maturity to understand what the experience is going to mean, and that is something only the dancer can decide. Young dancers seem more mature to me than nondancers of the same age. The concentration and discipline of dance have a way of making you grow up fast—fast enough, perhaps, so that you will know when you are capable of dealing with a large city, both as a dancer and as a person.

Study in a major ballet center means that the young dancer is in the company of very good dancers, some of them close to becoming professionals, and in advanced classes, of students who are already working dancers. You are plunged into daily comparisons—how well you with your seven years of training measure up to that dancer from the opposite side of the country with the same seven years behind him or her. This is a valuable experience, but be aware that you're not in dance class to get a grade. It is not worthwhile to expend mental energy and concentration comparing yourself favorably or unfavorably with the dancer working beside you. You have a greater responsibility in class, and that is to yourself—how well *you* are developing as a dancer, what *you* are learning, what *you* can do better today than you could do yesterday, what the teacher is teaching *you* that is new and challenging, whether *you* can meet the challenge.

A good teacher, however large the class, will have time for you. He or she will see what you are doing, will correct you, answer your questions, advise you on your strengths and weaknesses. And you have to take the responsibility to seek information not just from the teacher, but from many sources—from other students, from viewing all the performances you can, from your own sense of yourself.

The New York experience can mean not only a giant step forward in terms of your dance technique, but also a concentrated course in self-knowledge and the image you have of yourself.

One excellent young dancer from the West came to study with me for the summer, with the intention of returning home in September to continue her studies with her hometown teacher. When the time came for her to think about leaving, she admitted that she could no longer consider it.

"It would be like taking a step backward," she told me. "I was thought of as pretty good at home, and probably a lot better than most of the dancers I studied and performed with. In New York there are so many good dancers, and I need them to inspire me. I know I want to dance professionally, I know I can compete, so I have to start here, not at home."

Another student with great ability remarked how much she had gained from her experience in the city. "But I really am homesick, so I'm going back to dance with the local group. But I have so much to add to what we'll be doing back home because I've studied here in New York."

A third young woman studied with me for the summer and decided to go to a college with a dance program so that she could get a degree and still continue to study dance. "I haven't decided yet what I want to end up doing, but there's been nothing like this chance to get so completely into dancing, taking class every day, twice a day."

There is a bottom line to all this study in New York. It is that you must be prepared to get the most for your money—the best teaching, the widest experience, the fullest opportunity to see performances and share information. You cannot do it by skimming the surface and never getting to the substance. If you can't live without dancing, then you will be willing to make the effort that a period of study in a major dance center requires.

Study Alternatives

If you don't want to go to a big city, or if you have only a limited amount of time, there are still possibilities for study outside your hometown. I've mentioned that many students do come to New York only for the summer months, but there are also summer schools, some with scholarship programs, for both ballet and modern dance. At the North Carolina School of Performing Arts, for example, a young dancer has exposure to performances, workshops, and a full schedule of five or six hours of daily work. Some companies in large cities around the United States have summer programs as well. At these the dancer has the opportunity to study with the company director and others who might be instrumental in inviting the dancer to be an apprentice with the company. Some colleges offer summer programs that are open to qualified dancers.

Only keep in mind that you have to investigate all the possibilities— and remember that to study in a summer program isn't meant to be a summer vacation. Your parents aren't sending you away to entertain you for the summer.

For some dancers, this may be the first time away from home in an atmosphere of hard work and discipline. It can be overwhelming, even if it isn't New York, and it does take a certain amount of maturity not to become discouraged. But if you commit yourself to a routine of study and understand that you are getting a positive result, you will be becoming a better dancer and building that very necessary image of yourself.

I should add another word about college dance programs. In my years as artist-in-residence in a college atmosphere, I encountered many students who had studied little or no dance previously but who were able to incorporate dance training successfully with their academic studies. Dance is now becoming an enormously popular art course in many colleges and universities, so much so that program directors have a hard time finding faculty to keep up with the demand.

And these dance programs are good. They aren't simply a fun course for the casually interested; they can develop good dancers. One vivid example is a young man who had, in his precollege years, been active in track and field but had never danced before coming to college. He studied with me for three years and made such progress, from wholly untrained beginner to technically accomplished dancer, that after graduation he was able to dance professionally. In addition, of course, he had a college degree and the possibility of a career in a field other than dance if he so chooses.

A college program is a wonderful alternative for dancers who want to combine dance and academic study. There are opportunities for performance that aren't available to the student in New York. Consider, for example, how readily and inexpensively, with the backing of a good technical crew, a dance group can put together a performance at a college, where auditoriums are available, an audience is at hand, and the opportunity to create choreography and experiment with movement is not hampered by considerations of the marketplace. And in a college dance program, the young dancer has the chance to study and experience both modern dance and classical ballet in the proportions he or she desires. Even for the dancers who don't want to carry training to its limit, but also don't want to abandon the years of training that have gone before, college dance programs make it possible to use what they know for their personal satisfaction.

Institutional Schools

Institutional schools, generally attached to a major ballet company, are a somewhat specialized form of ballet training. No hard-and-fast rules apply to all of them: some require auditions for all students, others audition only potential scholarship students. Some have strict age limits: some feel that by the mid-teens, after several years of study, the dancer is set in his or her ways and it is not worthwhile to retrain the person to conform to the school's philosophy.

One way of judging the quality of an institutional school is whether or not the students in large part eventually graduate into the company to which the school is attached (in theory, this is why the school exists—to train dancers for the company). If the company isn't large enough to absorb all the school's graduates, do they then find positions with other major companies or are they able to go abroad to dance? For a school attached to a company subsidized by a city or state (in effect, by taxpayers' money), certain standards must be maintained because both school and company are responsible to the community. Such schools are worth looking into, if this is the experience the young dancer wants.

You can find out from your local teacher, or from various dance publications, when institutional schools are sending out adjudicators to studios or towns in your area to seek nominees for their scholarship programs. It may be worth a bus trip to be seen by the adjudicator coming to your area.

I hold no special brief for the School of American Ballet, but since I danced with its company, the New York City Ballet, for so many years, I share some of its dance philosophy, and I am often asked about the school by young dancers who think of it as the ultimate in dance training. True, it is one of the most famous institutional schools, and it has achieved a status close to that of a national school of dance (while happily detached from government bureaucracy, as is not the case with national schools in other countries).

It is, in a sense, a privilege to be accepted by the School of American Ballet, because acceptance comes on the basis of auditions, and most auditioning students are seen on the basis of recommendations, either by teachers the school has confidence in or by adjudicators who have scouted dancers throughout the country.

The School of American Ballet does have strict standards; it does prefer able students who are younger rather than in their later teens (the problem again of the student who has been trained in ways, however excellent, that do not meet the needs and philosophy of the school). It is seeking quality, but quality that will produce a dancer who fits in with the company. The school enters a student at a class level, and he or she is expected to make steady progress toward graduation. In addition, the young dancer is still attending high school while working a five- or six-hour day dancing.

It requires real dedication, the ability to absorb the pressure of different levels, and to conform to the standards and requirements of the school. It isn't the same comparatively independent life of the student studying in open classes. The end result, of course, is what matters. The direction of the teaching is toward the company; some ninety percent of the company is made up of graduates—and the New York City Ballet is a company with the longest continuous residency in an American city, with more performances in the city annually than any other. Graduates who do not dance with the New York City Ballet are sought by other major companies, here and abroad. They are well-trained (true of any good institutional school), adaptable to any artistic director's choice of repertoire.

The cost of the School of American Ballet is not appreciably greater than studying in open classes at a private studio a comparable number of classes per week. Shoes, when a dancer is studying not just technique, but pointe, variations, and *adagio*, can be expensive, when four or so pairs of pointe shoes are needed each month. A paying student must, of course, take into account living expenses as well as tuition; scholarship students (and most scholarships now seem to be granted on the basis of financial need rather than talent) may receive financial assistance beyond tuition.

I think the young student who wishes to attend an institutional school (or his or her parents) ought to investigate the requirements, in consultation with the local teacher, write for information, and take a close look at the financial aspects, the living situation that will be available to the dancer, and the arrangements for continuing academic education (early graduation, correspondence and extra assignments, professional schools are some possibilities).

The Dancer and the Family

So often I have heard from students: "It's hard to make my parents believe—really believe—that dance is what I want. They don't understand my need, they don't think it's possible to make a life in dance. They hated the idea that I had to go away to study."

I think the life of a creative artist always has opposition from people who don't "understand" the desire that drives the individual to paint, to write, to play an instrument. It is doubly difficult for the dancer, because dance manifests itself in very specialized circumstances—on a stage, before an audience. You can't entertain the neighbors quite so readily as, say, the pianist can.

Yet by the example of your sincerity and dedication to dance, and the sense of responsibility toward what you want to do, it is possible to overcome opposition.

"I used to be just someone who had this crazy idea she wanted to dance," one of the young women studying with me said. "It was as if my parents didn't want to admit that anything good could come out of me being in New York and studying dance.

"But something's happened. I persuaded them to let me come, I've worked hard, and now I go home and I'm referred to with pride as 'the dancer.' They've seen I'm serious, that this is what I really want, it's the only thing that makes me happy. And they've accepted that as a valid path for me. It's taken a long time."

Again, we are back to the dancer's responsibility: to learn, to find challenges, to make discoveries about dance and the self, to be a dancer in your own eyes and the eyes of others. And most important, to be that *person* who wants to dance: "I am that person who loves to dance, in my eyes, in my mother and father's eyes."

The force of your conviction can shape their conviction, and we are talking again of the communication that is so necessary. Can you, even at a young age, convince your parents that the experience is a vital and valuable one? You will encounter opposition to your desire at every turn—if not from your family, then from your peers. Girls will be told that dance has no future beyond taking classes for their entertainment value, or perhaps to learn "grace." Boys will be hard pressed to justify the preference for expressing physicality in dance rather than in contact sports. How difficult it can be for a young man to explain that America's premier male dancers are as manly a group as our most distinguished lawyers, doctors, and business executives.

I don't know that my mother ever truly understood the passion that underlay my determination. I don't know that any dancer, then or today, can convey to a nondancer what it means *to have to dance*. I know that when I became a performer, she and the rest of my family enjoyed the rewards of my work (although I never thought of it as hard work), and they were proud of me. They loved to see me dance, and they accepted the fact that dance was the road to happiness that I had chosen. But I think that most young dancers have to face the fact honestly: unless you are from a family which has a devotion to dance, you will always face some opposition—not necessarily overt, but the unspoken idea that you might be wasting your time, that you are accomplishing nothing of enduring value, that, in the end, you will never earn a living from your efforts.

Even a dancing family is no guarantee of perfect understanding. I recall my daughter, who is a dancer, saying to her father: "You've been around dance all your life and you lived with Mother all these years, but you still don't know what it means to dance." And my husband, who has indeed been associated with the dance world for many years, is the first to agree that it is true.

Although it is my intention here to speak as a dancer to other dancers, I think parents of young dancers can profit by knowing that our special world of dance is real and meaningful and the very core of our existence. Arguments do not alter the case, but perhaps the determination to dance and the fulfillment dancers gain are together worthwhile achievements—and worth understanding.

4

THE
DANCE CLASS

Taking class is a fact of every dancer's life, whether you are a beginner, an intermediate student, an advanced student on the brink of a career as a dancer, or a professional who performs with a major dance company.

The experience most intimately involved in my life is, of course, ballet class. Of necessity, I must focus on ballet, but although modern dance class does not follow the same kind of formal structure as ballet class, and each modern teacher has his or her own methods and point of view, I do believe it is still the dancer's responsibility to *take*, whatever the form of dance. And taking from a teacher in a class has to do with openness of attitude. The details may be different, but if you are truly a dancer, you are studying to perfect the instrument—and that is what all dance classes are intended to do.

Frustration is always a possibility for any dancer. When you can't get something and want to cry or scream, just think of all the adrenalin you are producing—that's more energy to make you able to work harder. Most dancers progress in sharp upward curves and then come to rest on plateaus where nothing seems to be happening until the next upward move starts. There's a period when the body takes time to absorb the discoveries of the nuances of movement and then it seems to reawaken, ready for new experiences.

A student of mine who had the opportunity to work for four weeks in an apprentice program with a ballet company and actually take part in performances came back to class and found, to her great discouragement, that she was making no progress beyond what she'd made in the performance experience.

"What's happening to me?" she asked. "Why can't I lift my leg higher, why can't I seem to get the pirouettes? Why am I having a problem technically, when things were coming so easily just a few weeks ago?"

What had happened (and it happens with professionals too, when they are working hard on a new piece with a choreographer) was that her concentration in getting ready for the performances had pushed her to a plateau. After the performances, she had to go through a time of settling down, while the muscles and the mind truly absorbed what she had learned.

Soon enough, she had begun a new upward move and the memory of that temporary discouragement faded. But every dancer has to be aware that he or she will suffer setbacks, perhaps fall apart for days, fail to make any noticeable progress. But with constant, concentrated work, the plateau is crossed and the body really knows what it has learned. The dancer is ready to make new discoveries.

Learn to live through the setbacks and the periods that seem to be without progress. Like a bad cold, they have to run their course, they can't be avoided, but knowing why they happen should make it possible for you to keep working, with the knowledge that things will certainly improve.

Ballet Class

If you are taking class in a small town in Ohio or a city in Texas, on the West Coast or the East Coast, you know what every other dancer taking class is doing—standing at the barre or at center practice doing *pliés, tendus, ronds de jambes, temps lié, grands battements,* and so forth. You are learning muscle memory, learning steps, learning combinations, getting closer to the hypothetical goal of every dancer, the perfect instrument, the performance that is the final fulfillment.

Wherever you go, the familiar pattern of ballet class is repeated. You can step into that well-known ("comfortable") world anywhere you go. There has to be a certain comfort in this fact, that you and every other dancer studying classical ballet use the same physical vocabulary; you practice the same movements; you speak the same language. There are no barriers to learning except those you might set up for yourself.

The common ground of ballet class that we all share makes it possible for me to speak to all ballet students about the nature of the classes that an intermediate or advanced student must take if he or she intends to have a career in dance, and at the same time make meaningful comments to students who haven't yet progressed that far. It is where they are headed, whether they are still learning vocabulary or are technically accomplished.

Everything you are doing now in class, at whatever level, is what you will be doing more intensively as your studies progress; everything you are doing is laying the groundwork of technique for future study. Everything you do is to a positive end.

A beginner may take class only once or twice a week; the more you want to dance, the more classes you will try to take. Sometimes, not surprisingly, the young dancer is limited not only by time but also by money—the people paying for those classes may not have quite the same devotion to dance. Parents may not understand the dancer's need, and may not have the money to provide as many hours of class as a dancer wants. This is a fact of a dancer's life, too, and if it's a harsh reality, it is also a test of the determination to dance. Can you do it, or can't you? Very early, you have to take a lot of responsibility on yourself, and go out and prove that you are serious and dedicated to dance.

Chance, someone remarked, seems to have played a large part in my career. Perhaps, but I believe you make your own chances through your desire and the wish to make the chances happen. Desire directs your intention, and lets you find the opportunity to study. You're in the right place at the right time. If you don't know or don't care that the opportunity is there, if you don't see it at all, you're not in line for the chance that changes your life. And you have to feel ready for the chance. You carry that feeling with you in the way you look—you can't fake that any more than you can your technique.

The point is, I think, that the desire to dance means that you take the responsibility of finding ways to study. No one forces the dancer to take class—not parents, a teacher, or peers. You have to be willing to take as many classes as you can to learn the vocabulary, as many classes as you can to prepare yourself to dance, not just to do the steps. And never forget the *person* who feels this way.

Kinds of Classes

How much class? What kinds? What to expect? How should you take a class? What should you be learning? What kind of progress should you make? How many hours a week should you be working?

You pick up this kind of information along the way from other students, and from teachers when you think to ask. There are real guidelines, however, although the question of progress and increased strength has partly to do with your physical development. A young teenager's body is changing rapidly. The older student may not be changing quite so fast, but the body continues to change into the twenties and later. Young men, starting at a later age, may develop faster than young women of the same age. Strength of back, legs, ankles, and feet can develop rapidly if you are working hard and properly. You can lose strength if you are forced to stop dancing by an injury, and you have to remember that the rebuilding process can take time—don't expect to be able to return to exactly the same stage you were at before the injury without a period of time regaining your strength.

The usual number of technique classes a young dancer ought to

consider is two classes a day, six days a week. These twelve classes are about the limit advisable for either a man or woman dancer, but each individual should be aware of what degree of physical activity the body can take. (You may also want to take classes in jazz or modern, mime, or even music.) A very young teenager, for example, would probably find this schedule too fatiguing—and besides, young people have other demands on their time and energy, such as school and social activities. And these are important for the well-rounded dancer, who is, after all, a person living in the world as well as in dance. In such cases, and for older students who might not be able to study full time, I'd suggest one class a day, five or six days a week (this in preference to, say, two classes a day, three days a week). I will speak later of what a full-time schedule of classes means, but I want to remind young dancers in the early stages of training that even if, for time or money reasons, they aren't able to take as many classes as they wish, it's essential to take whatever classes they can with the attitude that it's both a privilege and a responsibility to be a dancer. Get the most from every class, and seek, as I did, the "chances" that make further study possible.

The young dancers I know personally have come to New York from various parts of the country to study intensively for as long as they are able. They plan on studying full time, and many of them are studying so that they will be able eventually to dance professionally. It's assumed that they have a number of years of training behind them, that they're proficient in the vocabulary of ballet, and that most likely they are among the best young dancers in their area and have had some opportunity to take part in performances at home. Although some classes for adult beginners are included at my studio, neither I nor the other dance schools in New York that cater to intermediate and advanced students want to participate in the frustrations of students who are simply not ready, either in terms of technique or maturity, to take on a stringent program of work. It is not fair to teacher, fellow students, or the dancer if he or she doesn't have the vocabulary and at least the beginnings of a sense of what dance is all about. You ought not to think of coming to New York or another major dance center unless you have had encouragement from your hometown teacher to extend yourself to an arena where you can test yourself against able dancers from the whole country. This means that you have probably had four, five, or six years of training, although progress depends on the individual.

Most serious students will spend some five hours a day in class, with some time off between classes. It is a rigorous (but it shouldn't be a painful) training. It's the equivalent of having a job or going to graduate school, in preparation to become a professional, whether or not one actually ends up being paid to dance.

The young woman dancer has to take class in four different areas in the course of the recommended twelve weekly classes—ballet technique, pointe technique, pointe variations, and partnering. Variations and partnering might be taken once a week, pointe one to four times a week, depending on the stage of training. The remaining classes will be ballet technique, which works out to at least one technique class a day. A teacher might suggest fewer pointe classes and more technique for dancers who need to improve their strength in that area. Many students only begin dancing on pointe regularly when they reach the level I'm speaking of, and it may take them a few weeks or months to acquire sufficient strength in back, legs, and ankles before they're able to work in pointe class, and then variations and partnering.

For men dancers, the same twelve-class schedule each week applies. They ought to have at least one class a week in partnering, and ideally a part of the technique class should be devoted to the special techniques required of men. Very few schools provide daily class for men alone, so in seeking out a studio, the male dancer should be sure that he has some opportunity during the course of a week to concentrate on his needs as a developing dancer. Of course, since men as a rule don't study pointe and pointe variations, they make up the difference with additional technique classes.

Ballet Technique Class

The familiar ballet class with barre exercises and center practice that all ballet dancers know ought never to become a mere repetition of what you did the day before. There is a difference between practicing technique and rehearsing, which *is* a kind of repetition to learn to dance a choreographer's statement. You can be "comfortable" with the structure of the class, but you should be aware that each day you are doing more than repeating vocabulary you already know—you are taking steps forward rather than doing steps in place.

Teachers have differing dance and teaching philosophies that they attempt to convey to their students, and usually it takes time to impart them. This is another argument against studio hopping, or even against dividing up one's class schedule between two or more studios. It is difficult for me, for example, to convey my philosophy to people who go to eight classes in other studios and take two in mine; they don't have a chance to experience the development and patience I try to build into my teaching. But however the teacher chooses to teach, the goal should be *related* to the development of the student and increasingly demanding of the student. Random teaching that jumps from one area to another in the course of succeeding days without an internal design for progress cannot be productive.

I can speak with certainty about what I think a technique class for the intermediate and advanced student should be. Although other teachers may differ in their approach, it is possible for the student to discern the logic behind any teaching, and I offer my reasons for constructing class as I do in the belief that you will understand what is meant by an internal design and a plan for related development in technique class.

THE BARRE

I believe in a very simple, repetitive barre. I don't want complicated movements to distract from the barre's function, which is to develop strength, lengthen muscles, and develop muscle memory and placement, as well as musicality. Most technical corrections are made at the barre. They are repeated day after day and fine-tuned to your progress in order to develop a correct memory in your muscles, so that when you come to center practice, you will not, in theory, have to think about technique, but will have a physical feeling. To help the dancer move quickly and with facility, I try to help the student lengthen muscles at the barre gradually over his or her period of study with me. Too many dancers have overdeveloped thighs, and no feeling for their organic center.

There can be energy even in *plié*.

MUSICALITY

A basic rhythm is imposed on every movement at the barre. This rhythm is arbitrary but logical for each different movement. After many classes, it becomes a natural part of each *glissade, plié, tendu,* and so forth. Musicality and an understanding of rhythm are important because every choreographer works to the demands of the music he has chosen in conjunction with his imagination, his ingenuity, and his concept of choreographic design. A dancer who has rhythmic security is free to understand and execute the choreographer's concept because he or she comprehends nuances of musical phrasing, absorbed from the rhythms of the vocabulary.

CENTER

Just as the barre is a kind of technical workshop, so the center is a dance workshop. It puts together all the words of dance vocabulary you practiced so carefully at the barre and makes phrases and sentences out of them.

I am insistent about this "vocabulary-to-sentences" analogy, because I have so often seen otherwise technically proficient dancers come to center and fail to move like dancers. I am convinced that it is because they are thinking of individual steps rather than the phrasing of these steps to make combinations and movements. Never think of a movement as a step. A step is only a word or a phrase whose total meaning and validity depend on how you use it in a sentence.

My center often begins with an *adagio,* slow, careful, and well-placed. The *enchaînements* teach the dancer to shift weight continuously, moving from the supporting working leg to the designing leg and back again. The dancer becomes accustomed to the immediate subtle change necessary for fluidity. The rest of the body is also placed to provide maximum balance, facility of movement, and purity of line.

Placement is vital to today's dancer. It is neither static nor rigid, but varies with each combination. It is related to where you are and where you want to go. For example, if you are doing a combination that finishes with a pirouette from fourth position, when you hit fourth position, your weight should be slightly forward on your front leg. You should always be able to feel the tops of both thighs and the strength of the back. Your back leg is there only to push up quickly into the position of the particular turn. If your weight is to the back, think of the extra effort required to get up into the position of the turn —and of all the room for error that extra effort allows. However, if you have placed your weight forward and correctly, you are immediately in position to turn.

I have students work continuously on placement so that it will become automatic. In fact, an understanding of placement, along with musicality, is what makes a student into a dancer.

I construct a class to focus on one aspect of dance technique each day, while still teaching a rounded class. I may begin the week with emphasis on elongated movement, *adagio*. As the week progresses, the class expands on the movement. I will enlarge the movements and use the long line in jumps. By the end of the week, the class is doing everything fast; pirouettes are accelerated, the tempi are accelerated, the dancers are doing large movements in fast time, and finally small *allegro* movements, faster pirouettes, very fast *petit allegro*, and *batterie*.

I build the center combinations to break down each aspect of the day's concentration (turns, small lateral movements, big jumps, little jumps, and so forth), ending with the totality of what is to be accomplished. This segment approach seems to offer the most learning potential, and helps the student progress from combination to combination without difficulty, until the class gets to the most difficult. Within any given two-week period, a class covers almost every aspect of dance and technique.

In open classes such as I teach, there is always a range of technical ability. Given a hypothetical standard, there are always those who are better than the standard, and those who are less good. Thus, a combination is broken down so that initially slower students and those familiar with the combination but not technically as strong as others will learn to read the combination, while the more proficient students can refine what they are doing.

Some complex combinations are designed to train dancers to "read" a choreographer. This ability is essential for professionals. Whatever the choreographer is designing, he is going to speak in dance vocabulary or demonstrate movement. The dancer must be able to reproduce that in a flash. The best dancers don't always get the best roles, but the quick reader of choreography is always considered. Even for dancers who don't want to become professionals, reading combinations and grasping them quickly is enjoyable and part of the whole experience of dance.

The technique class is not, I should add, divorced from the matter of artistry. Artistry is a natural function of confidence, and when you can technically dance a combination, your body is free to express itself. This is what technique class and all the special classes I will discuss later are aiming for. Artistry comes from within, and it is manifested through the technique the dancer works so hard on. Artistry is the sum total of the dancer's self as a person; technique gives the dancer the fluency to express who that person is.

How to Take a Class

As mentioned, all dancers tend to work upward to plateaus, then remain there for a time before beginning to progress again. The plateaus can be frustrating, and so often I hear young dancers (as I did myself in my time) complain of having had a "bad" class, where nothing seemed to happen. The dancer has to be aware that such classes are not necessarily "bad," but contrasts to other days of work. You have to evaluate for yourself why a class was not productive, why you felt you didn't respond, and whether there was actually something you did gain.

In dance class, there are immediate consequences and long-range consequences. You have to trust in your teacher and believe in the long-range consequences, and not be overly concerned if the immediate consequences don't measure up. A bad class, too, has a lot to do with the way a dancer feels—there may be emotional stresses from the world outside the classroom, a lack of sleep, poor health. Learn to understand why, in addition to the plateaus, you may be having difficulties, and take steps to correct the reasons.

If you have trouble reading combinations, try saying them first out loud to yourself. Then walk through them, still repeating them out loud. Keep in mind what you want to do technically and how you

Sometimes students learn combinations by watching, sometimes by doing.

want to place your body. Next dance the combination tentatively, then more fully—and then just dance. Don't worry about falling on your face; you must train yourself to let go and trust your muscle memory. You never really fall.

Listen to the corrections your teacher gives you, and always try a correction immediately to transfer it from your head to your body. Listen to *everyone's* corrections. If the teacher is correcting another student, try the same thing yourself, off to the side. I suggest too that dancers keep a notebook in their dance bag to note down corrections after class so they won't be forgotten.

A teacher will respond to intention, to the dancer's effort and the way he or she accepts a correction and tries to make it work. A correction doesn't have to work the first time, or the second or third, but you keep on trying it. Mr. Balanchine once said to me, when I was working on a correction I couldn't seem to get and was becoming discouraged, "If you keep trying, in ten years you may have it. But if you never try, you'll never have it." (I had it down in six months.) This is the way a young dancer should approach corrections.

If you find you cannot handle a combination (and in an open class, the combinations may be designed to challenge a higher level technically than you have reached), don't be discouraged. Instead, narrow your goals. Concentrate on one aspect of the combination and learn that. If you accomplish that, you will have gained something, and you will be in a position to deal with another aspect of the combination in a subsequent class.

It is the student's responsibility to *take* from the teacher, as much as it is the teacher's to give. If you don't understand a correction, if you have questions, you should be able to ask freely, either during the class or after. This is your absolute right, and an obligation to yourself. Dancers are selfish as far as their work is concerned, and the young dancer must learn to be so. It is not merely a matter of learning to dance properly, but it can be of vital importance to the dancer's physical well-being. A correction or a movement improperly understood can mean an injury that will keep you from dancing for a long period, and at the risk of sounding terribly ominous, could end your training and hopes as a dancer permanently.

I have talked at length about your attitude as you learn from your teacher in class. But a dancer is also a person living in a big, exciting, demanding world outside of class, and both facets of existence have to be taken into account and made to coexist without conflict.

Remember that you have to walk into a classroom and make it a cocoon. You forget the argument you just had with your friend; you put aside the distractions and pressures of hurrying to get to class and getting practice clothes in order, the rent that has to be paid, the illness in the family. If you don't, you will not be concentrating on what you are doing in class.

Class is, in a sense, the performing dancer's world in microcosm. When you are a professional appearing before an audience and attempting to express your artistry the best way you can, you can't be anything but a dancer dancing. For those moments, you aren't son, daughter, wife, husband, mother, or father, but a *dancer*. You have to take responsibility for your life outside of dance, of course, and it's sometimes more difficult than the life of a nondancer, but the ability to shift gears is essential. When my children were small, I was performing regularly with the company. Once, my son fell seriously ill on a day when I had a major performance. I spent the day doing everything that had to be done for his sake—doctors and medication and care. Then I went to the theater, put on my costume and makeup, and danced the evening's performance—as a dancer. When I came offstage, I was a mother again with a different focus of concern. This is not an unfeeling or irresponsible attitude; knowing how to focus, how to organize is the way of a performing artist's life. The student dancer must take class with the same attitude, and not be overwhelmed by distractions so that the period in class is wasted by a lack of concentration. I do believe, though, the ability to focus that the discipline of dance gives you carries over into all aspects of life. You have to practice it, of course, just the way you practice technique, but it stands you in good stead in everything you choose to do.

Pointe Class

A dancer works on pointe when she has developed technically to the point where the ankles are strong, and the muscles of the legs and back can support her body. You don't dance *on* the toes; you should never feel your toes on the floor with pain. They should never hurt. You feel pressure but not pain. You support yourself on pointe because of the strength of other parts of the body—thighs, back, hip placement.

The dancer herself isn't able to make the decision about when she is ready to dance on pointe. The teacher sees when she is ready to make the transition from half pointe in ballet slippers to toe shoes. It is not, in other words, for the student to say, "I am ready to work on pointe." Rather, it is for her to ask the teacher, "*Am* I ready for pointe?" The teacher can judge when leg muscles have developed and when the back is strong enough.

Going to pointe before a dancer is ready can be detrimental. If proper strength is lacking, too much pressure is put on the feet and ankles (this should *never* happen), and the result may be a chronic injury, such as sprained ankles, bunions, soft corns. Tendonitis (or tendinitis) is also a possibility when the dancer isn't strong enough to support herself on pointe or when she hasn't been taught where the balance of the body over the toes is.

A teacher uses his or her experience to make judgments about a student's strength and ability, but some of the considerations for being ready for pointe are these:

When there is enough development in the calves, thighs, and back so that the student can do advanced ballet technique.

When she feels comfortable jumping, has speed in *brisés,* and is comfortable doing *grands jetés.*

When the ankles are strong enough to move quickly and to do *petit allegro* without sprains.

When the lower back feels comfortable always when she jumps.

It usually takes three or four years of training to reach the strength necessary for dancing on pointe, and sometimes longer. This doesn't mean that pointe work is extended only to advanced students, however. When a young person—even an eleven- or thirteen-year-old with sufficient training and strength—is developing her dance technique, the natural development is to gradually introduce the dancer to pointe. This is done by allowing her to work fifteen minutes or so after ballet class on pointe to familiarize the body with the extended leg that pointe means.

Some students need more time to develop their muscles, and aren't ready for pointe until the mid-teens. The rate of the body's growth is a factor in the teen-age years, and not everyone develops at the same rate. The young dancer shouldn't be discouraged if it seems that she is behind the other students in physical strength. She will catch up soon enough if she works on ballet technique and allows her body time to grow. For those who love to dance, the idea of going to pointe is exciting, but if you are more interested in having those toe shoes than in doing it properly, you've missed something in understanding what dancing is all about.

Pointe work is not something different from half pointe, but an extension of ballet technique when properly taught. I always fall back on the image of the toe shoe being like a glove; it is a dressing for the foot as well as an added support.

Many of the young women dancers who come to study with me have done some pointe work with their hometown teachers and have perhaps danced on pointe in local performances. They may not, however, be fully prepared to take regular pointe technique class. If they have had some experience on pointe, I will often suggest that they wear an old pair of pointe shoes for center practice in ballet technique class to give them a feel of the difference this type of shoe makes. Although worn shoes can't support the dancer on her toes, they are more supportive than ballet slippers, and she can familiarize herself with the difference in feeling and weight and balance.

Before dancers are ready for pointe technique class, I find it helpful to spend fifteen or twenty minutes at the end of ballet class working with them on pointe. In three months or so (and often less), they are strong enough to be comfortable on their toes for an extended period and thus able to complete a full pointe class. The development of students working toward pointe class in the short segments after ballet class is usually rapid because it is an extension of what the dancers are already doing in technique class. There is also the added factor of *wanting* to dance on pointe, and the sense of comfort they acquire in toe shoes. I was able to go to dancing on pointe after only about two years of study because I was fortunate in having a good teacher who helped me develop a strong back and a good jump. I immediately felt more comfortable on pointe than I did on half pointe, a feeling that continues to this day.

When a dancer takes a pointe technique class (anything from one to four times a week), she is aiming at strengthening her ankles and thighs and finding an extended new center to her body. Such a class is taught differently from a regular ballet class; the preparations to rise on pointe are different from preparations to get on half pointe in ballet slippers because we have to extend to the tip of the toes. When a dancer is on pointe, she has a more extended line than on half pointe, and there is a greater sense of the extension of muscles in the thighs, back, legs, and feet. Jumping on pointe has a different feeling. It is much lighter; you must hold your body more lightly when you have only the tip of the toes to land on, and not the whole ball of the foot.

If the dancer on pointe does not feel strength in her ankles, something is wrong. If she doesn't feel the extension of her body and that her center is changed from half pointe, something also is amiss. When you hit a pose such as an arabesque or a *retiré* position, the body has a different center—you are balancing from the tips of your feet rather than the balls of your feet.

The pointe technique class, then, gives the dancer exercises and techniques for strength, for discovering the extended center of the body over the toes, and for developing the ability to dance with the extended line that pointe allows. The pointe class brings the dancer closer to the performance experience of classical vocabulary.

If it happens that you are a dancer who has trained for six or so years and find that when you get on pointe, even with properly fitting shoes, you are not comfortable, and after giving it a fair test, you believe that you will never be as comfortable as breathing dancing on your toes—that pointe work doesn't give you a new sense of yourself—then I think you should look elsewhere for an arena in which to dance. There are many opportunities. With a background in classical dance and with the strength and knowledge it has given you, you can transfer your energies and dedication to modern dance, for example. Martha Graham, after all, and many of the innovators of modern dance, felt that ballet was too restrictive for their vision, and they took off their shoes to dance barefoot and use their feet in a different way—to international acclaim.

Although these comments on pointe classes have been directed to young women dancers, I should interject that although male dancers don't generally perform on pointe (Ashton's Donkey Variations in *A*

Midsummer Night's Dream and Lichine's Devil in *Fair at Sorochinsk* were, however, choreographed for men on pointe), some young men do study pointe for the great strength it can give to feet and ankles. They often find that it adds a dimension to their dancing by giving them a feeling of their extended arch from having risen on their pointes, as well as a different feeling of line.

Variations Class

In the process of taking pointe technique class, the dancer should also begin to experience choreography on pointe. She should be strong enough to do simple variations that are comprised of combinations of vocabulary put together to make a statement in dance.

The variations class and what the dancer experiences there are very, very important. For the aspiring professional, the class is an essential training ground for the future; for any young dancer, learning variations means she is truly *dancing*, whether or not she is seeking a career in dance. In short, dancing variations is as much fun as it is hard work.

In variations class, the dancer is required to take a combination of movements and put them together to make a complete statement with a beginning, a middle, and an end. It's like the actor who memorizes a scene from Shakespeare or the pianist who takes the chords and scales that have been practiced over and over again and puts them together to play a piece by Schubert. In ballet, we take a forty-five-second or one-minute or three-minute combination of movements, often from a major ballet where a choreographer has created a statement in dance, and try to reproduce it. The dancer is not only doing steps and practicing technique, she is also discovering the nuances of how one movement balances another; she is becoming aware of musicality with different timing and rhythm. Experiencing the style of a variation from a Tchaikovsky ballet is going to be very different from one to Stravinsky's music—even if you are using the same steps for both.

Highlights of great ballets—*Swan Lake, Sleeping Beauty, Nutcracker,* modern classics such as *Agon, Apollo,* or *Four Temperaments* —are the materials studied and performed in variations class. Some teachers use variations that have been established in performance, others choreograph their own variations, and some take a piece of music not used in a familiar ballet and choreograph it on a dancer or group of dancers, which provides the added experience of learning the music as well as the choreography. For variations classes, this can be a much more valid learning experience.

If the teacher who has been a professional dancer has actually danced the variation in performance, he or she brings to the class a depth of understanding of the choreography that an otherwise good teacher who has never performed doesn't always have. Remember that in variations class, dancers are closest to the performance aspect than in any other class. The teacher who has had the opportunity to experience the different styles of movement designed by various choreographers can perhaps better convey the subtleties of the variation. What the teacher may have danced onstage before a live audience includes not only the steps and the style of the choreographer, but the subtleties and nuances experienced through performance.

Variations class teaches the dancer how to learn choreography quickly; it builds up stamina, it enables her to share the experience of what she may have seen other dancers perform onstage. If you know the music, and have actually learned to dance a variation to it, you are in a better position to get a job. You may, for example, have learned a *Nutcracker* variation in class, and be asked to dance in a performance of the ballet. Even if the choreography is different, the fact that you have experienced one interpretation will help you with another because you are aware of the nuances of the music; you've actually danced a piece of choreography to that music.

This flexibility is part of learning to be a dancer, and it connects firmly with the dancer's career. I first learned the Royal Ballet version of *Swan Lake*, which I danced with the National Ballet of Canada. Later, I was invited to dance *Swan Lake* with a different company, with different choreography. It took me three or four days to adjust to the different steps, but since I had already done one solid version, I had an interpretation of the role and a knowledge of the music. The hard work came down to the limited time I had to rehearse the new version. I had a similar experience with *Coppélia*, and in a slightly different context, *Les Sylphides*, which I had danced in at the beginning of my career as a corps member. When I first danced the lead some years later, the director asked me where I had learned the role. I explained that I had participated in the ballet long before and had learned the music and the romantic style of *Les Sylphides*.

Once you have learned a version of a ballet, it's easy to change to another; once you have experienced a variation, you have confidence that you can actually perform it; once you know a style of choreography, you can apply it to new situations. You know that you don't dance a variation from *Swan Lake* the way you would a variation from *The Firebird*. And the teacher who has experienced the differences in performance has, I think, another dimension to convey to his or her students.

Besides choreography, what do you learn about dancing variations?

I received some good advice from Mr. Balanchine about how to approach a variation, which I followed throughout my dancing career and try to give my students. He told me, in effect, that when a dancer starts the variation, it must be very exact, very much as though she were shouting, "Here I am!" to catch the audience's attention for the minutes she would be dancing alone before them. The finish, too, must also be exact, like putting a period to the statement that has just been made.

"Whatever happens in between doesn't matter," he added. "You can fall down and the audience won't remember."

He was trying to convey that the beginning of a variation has to present what you are going to say, and the finish has to explain what you have said. What happens in between is not "steps," but a joining of that beginning and that end with meaningful phrases. The strong beginning carries the dancer through the phrases; the intention stated initially gives shape and continuity to the middle, and the logical development, with a strong finish, keeps the dancer from faltering, even though she may be tired by the end.

In variations class, I try to guide students who are not experienced professionally to use a strong beginning and end to variations to make the middle an integral part that ties them together, and not just "filler." The beginning and end create continuity that helps carry them through the variation.

Remember that the young dancer in variations class is not just reproducing technique and poses, but is learning how to phrase movement, and how it relates to music. He or she is experiencing what *dance* is, and how the movements are connected in actual choreography. The experience is vital for any dancer, because performance, whether as a professional or not, is why you are shaping your desire to dance and the passion for your art by your training.

Musicality and Choreography

I believe that musicality in a dancer can make the difference between a genuine dancer and one who is merely technically proficient. Ideally, a young dancer, and especially one who wants to dance professionally, ought to study music theory and practice for at least a couple of years. Unless you are innately musical, you need to develop a strong concept of musicality and timing to help you grasp the physicality of the phrasing of movement more readily.

Dance is pretty much inseparable from sound in the contexts we know (even though dance can be highly effective without music in its theatrical form). An understanding of music seems essential for the dancer. If time or money prevents you from actual study of music, you have to at least keep your ears and mind open—to expose yourself to performances, both of ballet and orchestral concerts.

When you see ballet, pay attention to more than the dancers' technique. So often I have heard young people after a performance comment on how a dancer balanced, how she did pirouettes, how cleanly she danced, but never a word on how she related to the sound she was dancing to. You can train yourself to listen as well as see; you can get a feeling for music and rhythms simply by turning on a radio or a phonograph. Music is not a frill for dance, but a partner, and often can be the inspiration for dance and for the quality of the performance.

The majority of great choreographers are those who have been able to join movement and music with memorable results, ballets that are enduring works of art. Many choreographers have been dancers in their time, but not all dancers are choreographers. Ballet students are seldom given the opportunity to experiment with putting movements together, to understand how to make statements in dance on their

A stretch can be completed within a frame of musical time.

own. For this reason, it is essential to study choreography through variations class.

I think it is a pity that ballet study doesn't include choreography, since choreography really forms the bridge between technique and actual dancing. Students of modern dance and creative movement often learn the practice of choreography to their advantage, but the classical ballet dancer seldom has the chance to do so, or to be guided through the creative process by an experienced teacher. Choreography, like dance, must be practiced. There are fundamentals to be learned; there are rules; there are ways to shape movement in space, whether you design it in diagonals or circles, front and back. I foresee a time when choreography will, in fact, be more widely taught to young dancers, now that dance is becoming such a basic cultural experience. Although opportunities today for choreographic study are still limited, if you want to know how to create movement, you have to take the responsibility for finding any opportunity available to practice.

One such opportunity is provided by the National Association for Regional Ballet, with its summer Craft of Choreography Conferences, held annually in different areas of the United States. Although the conferences are designed for young choreographers who have acquired a foundation in the art, rather than for beginners, they do offer a unique chance for the choreographer to work with an experienced staff and to experiment with a wide range of dance and musical styles, as well as to be exposed to discussions of other aspects of dance—costuming, lighting, staging, and so forth.

Since a number of dancers also participate in the conferences, they provide a mutual learning experience that isn't available in the usual classroom or with the pressure of preparing a company for performance. The dancers are given a chance to work with several choreographers, which serves to extend their abilities to read choreography; the choreographers have a group of trained dancers on which to design ballets and other forms of dance.

Partnering Class

When I was a young dancer in the early years of my career, my only experience dancing with a partner was in performing choreographed works with the companies I danced with. I had never actually studied the technique of dancing with a male partner, and I realize now that because of my lack of background in partnering, I was uncomfortable in those early years. Instead of taking the responsibility for my lack of knowledge on myself—there were almost no partnering classes, so how could I be blamed?—I always blamed uncomfortable moments or mistakes on my partner. Partnering, in any case, was something a dancer had to learn through experiencing it, by trial and error, but it didn't seem too difficult. The man was there to lift and support; the woman could rely on him, and more than rely—could lean on him.

About this time, and long before equality between the sexes became a popular issue, I received a lesson that I've made a permanent part of my dance philosophy. André Eglevsky joined the New York City Ballet and invited me to dance with him in concerts outside the city. It was an exciting chance for me to dance a complete *pas de deux* with a very distinguished male dancer. We began rehearsing, and one day Mr. Eglevsky stopped in the middle of our beginning *pas de deux*.

"You know," he said, "you must dance alone."

I didn't know what he was talking about. We started out dancing together, he danced a solo variation, then I did, and then there was a coda where we danced separately and together to make a finale. For at least half of the *pas de deux*, I wasn't dancing "alone" at all—he was there lifting and supporting me. That's the way partners worked.

"You have to understand," he said to my blank look, "that after we dance together, I have to go out and dance a variation by myself. I want to do it well, not tired out because my partner has taken up my energy from the *pas de deux*."

For the first time, I saw what it meant to be a real "partner." I had to do my share, even when he and I were dancing together. I couldn't tire him for his solo, when he was going to display his technical prowess, by requiring him to support me when we were together—so *I* could save myself for my solo.

Partnering is a fifty-fifty relationship. The man is there to dance *with* the woman, not to support her and do most of her work. Even when they are dancing together, the woman must be dancing "alone," strong enough to support herself without falling back on her partner's strength. And as part of that partnership, the male dancer must know every step that she takes, every movement, so that he can complement her, lift her properly, dance *with* her.

Partnering shouldn't be studied until the young woman can support herself on her own pointe and is able to do two double pirouettes, *tendu, relevé,* and *changement* on pointe alone. Only then can she begin to learn to be an effective and equal partner.

Young dancers who come to New York to study have seldom studied partnering in their home communities, unless they have participated in regional ballet, although they may have taken part in performances where male dancers were required to lift and hold women. Partnering is an important area of study for dancers who want to enter today's competitive dance market. Even for those who don't intend to make dancing a career, dancing with a partner is another level of enjoyment that ought to be experienced once technique is strong enough, just like dancing on pointe and doing variations.

As soon as I learned my lesson from Mr. Eglevsky, I sought out partnering classes, to learn in a systematic way what I had been picking up hit or miss.

Students involved in a full-time schedule of training should, as soon as they are ready, include a class in partnering each week. For men, of course, training in partnering is essential, since classical ballet requires them to learn how to lift a woman partner properly, without injuring themselves, and with grace and an awareness of the woman's movements. But it is equally important for a woman dancer, as I have explained. If dancers have to learn to be selfish about their art, it applies equally to men and women, and both must understand why and how the other dances.

Partnering is a fifty-fifty relationship. Left, rehearsing with Mr. Balanchine and André Prokovsky.

Rehearsing with Mr. Balanchine and Herbert Bliss.

Man or Woman Teacher?

The exceptional teacher of either sex is what any young dancer wants. The quality of communication in teaching and the ability to bring out the individual natural grace of the dancer are more important than whether men are taught by a man, women by a woman.

I was fortunate to have a woman teacher at one point who taught me to do nearly all a male dancer has to do by training, such as double *tour* and double *saut de basque,* multiple pirouettes, and jumps. There are some male teachers who couldn't successfully teach a woman this. For a male dancer who is an advanced student wanting to refine his technique, perhaps study with a male teacher is more productive if the teacher is experienced enough to communicate the special combinations the male dancer's role requires. On the other hand, a woman teacher may have that same ability to communicate to the male dancer, and also give him added grace to his movements, as an example, through *port de bras.*

I do believe that for the most part, an experienced woman teacher is best for teaching young women to work on pointe, although Mr. Balanchine and Mr. Volkoff had great understanding. There is a definite technique involved in working on pointe that can best be conveyed by someone who has done it (always acknowledging the exceptional women teachers who have never danced on pointe and still produce beautiful dancers). It is the exception rather than the rule that men teach pointe work, since they have not had the experience and don't therefore understand the questions of center of balance and technique that are involved, and the timing needed to get on pointe.

We come back to our starting point: the quality of the teacher— whether a man or a woman—is the most important consideration. The chemistry, the inspiration, the clarity of the teaching, the sense of progress and growing strength the teacher gives the dancer—these are significant factors, especially in the early stages of training. And as the dancer grows in intelligence about dance, he or she will take the responsibility for seeking out the teachers who can provide the best training. In my studio, for example, many young men take class from me—and from my colleagues at the studio, who are men. The same is true of many of the young women, who take ballet class and study pointe with me, but include in their schedule classes with the men teachers.

Cost of Classes, Scholarships

The cost of taking class twelve times a week can be high. The dancer with a full schedule is going to be wearing out expensive shoes at a rapid rate, along with possibly living away from home in a strange city where the detail (and expenses) of everyday living aren't automatically taken care of.

Any young dancer who plans to spend time in a city like New York must take into account all the many expenses he or she will be facing. Studios will give you their class rates (in some cases, a discount for buying a dance card for a quantity of classes). City rents are high, food is high, transportation is yet another cost, all in addition to practice clothes and shoes. Don't believe that you can necessarily support yourself by working in addition to studying (in a later chapter, I will talk about how young dancers perceive the problems of coping in New York), although it is possible to supplement your money by some work. Make a real effort to understand what the cost is going to be, and what support you can get from your family.

Some teachers will give scholarships to promising students who aren't able to afford as many classes as they want. It has always seemed to me that students who have shown an outstanding ability to learn and a real determination to dance are as worthy of scholarship consideration as technically advanced students who seem to have less drive to succeed. If you are given the opportunity to take class without payment as a scholarship student, you do have a special responsibility to set an example, in a sense, for the other students, and to justify the consideration given you by demonstrating a serious focus on your work.

I can give no firm answers about how to support yourself and your dancing—I do believe that the will shows you the way. The adventure of discovering how you can afford to study dance is part of the discovery of what it means to be a dancer.

Movement needs energy.

5

SHOES, CLOTHES AND OTHER NECESSITIES

All ballet dancers talk about shoes. They spend money and time looking for just the right shoes. Shoes, especially toe shoes, are actual extensions of the dancer's feet, and as such they really are a vital part of the dancer's life. How important? Enough, I think, for every young dancer to know all about how to buy them, what to look for, how they should feel, how to care for them, and even what the wearing of them can tell about how the dancer is dancing. The dancer is not alone in his or her interest in correct shoes: craftsmen devote their lives to making ballet and toe shoes, with much of the construction being done by hand; and the companies who produce the shoes dancers wear and make them available in the marketplace are always trying to make better shoes.

A somewhat unique relationship exists between manufacturer and user, possibly because the dancer's needs are so individual and specialized that it behooves the manufacturer to provide as close to a comfortable ideal as possible. I participated in the process shoe manufacturers go through a couple of years ago when a major company, interested in making another style of shoe, came to me to act as a consultant. The company has a wide range of shoe styles to suit dancers with a variety of foot conformations (long toes, short toes, normal heels, small heels, arched and nonarched feet), and I myself had worn their shoes as a performer for some twenty years. I later found it necessary to switch to the shoes of another company, which I continued to wear until I concluded my performing career.

The company wanted to know what the difference was between the shoe of theirs I wore for twenty years and the one I was wearing at the time I retired. It is difficult to express in words what is basically a sense of feeling and comfort, but it was very evident to me that as I became more experienced as a dancer, my foot was constantly changing with the work. It became more sensitive the longer I worked; what I eventually needed in a shoe was something different from what I needed initially. The suggestions I gave the manufacturer were incorporated in a series of sample shoes that were tested by my students, many of whom found them more comfortable than the shoes they were accustomed to wearing.

Be aware that even if you have worn a toe shoe successfully for a few years, your feet do change with the development of the body and the strength of the feet. You can't assume that you will always wear the same style of shoe, and you have to be aware of changes that might be occurring in the feet and body, requiring a new style. Company dancers, of course, often have shoe lasts made to their feet alone to get the best fit possible, but even they, working on pointe every day, have to remain alert to possible changes in their feet.

It is a popular misconception among nondancers that dancing on pointe is somehow "unnatural," impossibly difficult, and perpetually painful. It is not at all. It's part of the development of a trained body, and the dancer feels perfectly comfortable dancing this way. Dancing on pointe should never be painful. Wearing toe shoes shouldn't be a painful experience either. Dancing on pointe must be like breathing; you cannot be in pain and also dance—dance is an expression of joy.

This is not to say that there is no pressure on the toes; there is. Nor does it mean that a dancer who goes to pointe for the first time will not encounter some aching muscles, sometimes even a blister before the skin toughens. But the ache disappears as the muscles adjust to the new center of balance in the body, and toe shoes should never be painful or even uncomfortable.

Buying Shoes That Fit

There are a couple of handy rules of thumb for buying shoes, whether they be toe shoes or ballet slippers: Get them from a reliable source, have them fitted by a person who is experienced with dance shoes, and do not be intimidated by the salesperson who says, "This is all we have; take your pick." More experienced dancers have a clearer idea of what they want and need. Young dancers too often settle for what seems to be available—unaware, perhaps, that there are many, many styles available from the six or so companies that make dance shoes, that the type of shoe you may need depends to a certain extent on the style of your training, and that what might have been suitable once no longer is because the foot has changed.

If you're allowed to try on only two pairs of shoes and neither is comfortable, be persistent and don't compromise. It can be dangerous to buy a pair of shoes to "make do." For this reason, it's wise to avoid emergencies when buying shoes. Take the time to try as many styles as necessary, and once you have found the right shoe, be sure to put the style on order so that the store will be getting them in for you on a regular basis.

In larger cities, there may be a number of stores that specialize in dance equipment, and they may have trained salespeople who understand what dance shoes are all about. Smaller cities and towns may have only a department store where dance shoes are available, and you may be lucky if you can find someone who understands how to fit dance shoes. Remember that you know your feet better than any salesperson, and you are able to feel your foot in the shoe, to tell whether or not it is held snugly (which doesn't mean tightly) and comfortably. You have to learn to trust your judgment, and you can get information and advice from your teacher. If your foot is very arched and the ankles are weak, you will likely need a more supportive toe shoe. A flexible sole allows the dancer to go through the metatarsal and allows the ankle to get strong, which is perhaps the ideal for a normal-shaped foot. But if you have need of more support—for reasons of foot conformation—your teacher may be able to suggest shoe styles that might be suitable.

Although ballet slippers and toe shoes are expensive and will become more expensive still, never allow yourself to be convinced that you can buy shoes to "grow into." Dance shoes must fit at once, just the way tennis shoes must if you're going to play well. Incidentally, size one is the smallest size now available in toe shoes from manufacturers. If the foot is smaller than that, the very young dancer probably is not ready to dance on pointe.

Ballet slippers shouldn't be too tight or too loose. When you go up on half pointe, they shouldn't cut the front of the foot where the toes meet the upper arch. If this is happening, you will not feel the balance of the body over the half pointe, and it will also push your back out of balance, as well as cause calluses and blisters. If you're aware of even mild pressure on the front of your foot, the slippers probably don't fit properly. Look carefully at the vamp of the shoe. It shouldn't be too high, and again should conform to the length of the toes.

One young man, who had been studying with me for two years and whose feet always looked beautiful in the pointing of the toes, remarked: "I'm having a problem with my feet constantly cramping." He'd been wearing the same style of ballet slipper all along, and said that when he moved and jumped off the floor, his feet felt perfectly all right; the shoes didn't seem tight at all.

"But when I'm standing at the barre," he said, "I get such cramps in my feet, it almost kills me."

It turned out that he had been wearing a ballet slipper that was too narrow. When the toes are pointed, there is a contraction (in his case, just enough so that the shoe did fit and the foot looked very good), but when the dancer stands flat on the foot, there is an expansion. In the young man's case, it was enough so that the narrow shoe no longer could accommodate the foot comfortably. A slight change in shoe width that didn't alter the look of his pointed toes prevented the cramps he had suffered for such a long time.

When you are wearing a properly fitting pointe shoe, you should feel comfortable whether standing on your toes or flat. The shoe, standing flat, is not too tight, but is still snug, and when you go up on pointe, you can go right from the metatarsal to the tips of your toes without curling them. Curling the toes may be the result of incorrect training. If you also curl your toes in your ballet slippers, it means that you have learned to grip with your toes when you dance—and you should dance with a complete foot. Curling the toes will contract the arch, and if the arch gets very tight, you will have a problem with tendonitis and then tightness of the calf. When it gets to that point, it's dangerous, because you will be working through constant pain. The result is likely to be a paralysis of the whole foot, a possible knee injury, or a torn ligament and excruciating pain.

If you work in toe shoes that seem to force you to curl your toes when you put them on, it may be that the shoes have too little space in the toes. Although constant use of such incorrectly fitting shoes can have the same result as the learned tendency to curl the toes, it can be corrected by getting a properly fitting shoe that will allow you to go through the metatarsal without gripping the toes.

When you are on pointe, you must feel that the tips of the toes are flat across, and you have balance. Almost no one has toes that are naturally straight across, however, so you have to choose the type of box that is right for the shape of your toes—square, flat, or pointed. The length of the vamp is also important in relation to the shape of the toes. If you have a large big toe and the other toes graduate down on a sharp diagonal, you have to be sure that the vamp is high enough to cover all the toes so that you have support across the metatarsal and the little toe is also supported. Check the underside of the shoe—the size of the pleats in the fabric where it connects to the sole are related to the length of your toes. If you have long toes, it will be difficult for you to go through your natural metatarsal if there is too much pressure because of short pleats. If you have short toes, it is impossible to go through the metatarsal if the pleats are long. For a short-toed person, the length of the pleats should not be more than an inch, measuring from under the platform to the sole. In many cases, when the toes are longer the pleats can be longer—an inch and a quarter or so.

When you stand on pointe in a pair of toe shoes, there should be a balance from toe to thigh to hip, and through the whole back, and the top of the knee should be straight. That is, you have a placement from the floor right up to your waist, and you have enough balance from the tips of your toes to feel that the tops of the knees are straight, right up through the spine to the top of your head.

The heel of the toe shoe shouldn't be loose, but at the same time it should not be so snug that you can feel excessive pressure on the heel that can cause a swelling at the back. In some instances, dancers have long toes and narrow heels. When they are standing flat in a toe shoe, it seems just snug enough; but when they get up on pointe, the heel will feel loose. This does not mean that the shoe is the wrong size; the problem can be taken care of by sewing elastics on the heel on each side of the seam (on the outside rather than inside, where the elastic might cause an irritation as the shoe moves up and down). On the other hand, a loose heel on a shoe that seems to be the right size means that you should keep trying other styles from different manufacturers until you find a style that conforms to your foot, both toes and heels. Again, don't be persuaded by a salesperson that the shoe will fit better "after you've worked in it."

This is not true. If it doesn't fit properly when you buy the shoe, it won't fit properly later. Keep looking and trying shoes until you are satisfied.

All toe shoe manufacturers label every pair of shoes with the name of the shoemaker who made them. But since each shoemaker has his own idiosyncrasies and most of the work is done by hand, a size 4½ AA made by one shoemaker will be at least slightly different in fit from a size 4½ AA made by another. Experienced dancers learn to ask for shoes by maker when they have found the style and maker who suits them. The inexperienced dancer usually buys stock shoes, rather than what manufacturers call "special order" shoes—orders by maker label. Special order shoes, unfortunately, cost somewhat more than stock shoes, but they are a necessary expense for the serious dancer.

If you are having a problem with stock shoes and need special order shoes, it is worth the money and effort. Be sure the head of the department puts in your order, and be prepared to wait even for a couple of months. Once the shoes come and you are satisfied with the style, put in a standing order, so that the special order shoes will be arriving regularly as you need them. This is especially important if you hope to be invited to participate in a performance while you are studying. You may have to wear old or stock shoes for class, but in performance, if you have to wear stock shoes, you won't dance as well, physically or psychologically, especially if you are comparatively inexperienced as well.

I have always believed that good preparation is ninety per cent of a dancer's success.

Once you have bought your dance shoes, don't hesitate to go back to the store where you bought them if they prove to be defective. This does happen often enough with toe shoes and ballet slippers to warrant a comment. The shoes are handmade from small batches of material. Even the shoemaker may not be aware that he has received a poor piece of leather, so that the seams of the finished shoe split after only a little wearing. When the shoe splits at the vamp after only a short time, the leather probably was not flexible and was pulled too tight in preparation for making the ballet slipper. Sometimes the satin in toe shoes is defective and the seams split, or the soles are crooked not because the shoemaker did a poor job, but because the raw materials happened to be inferior. I believe the store and the manufacturer have to accept the responsibility for defective goods, even though it was not an intentional attempt to pass on inferior shoes. You should expect to have the shoes replaced—but be aware that dance shoes wear out very fast with use, perhaps in a week and a half or less for a serious student (and more rapidly for performers). It's a problem no one has found an answer for.

About Ballet Slippers

The soft ballet slippers worn in the earlier stages of training by girls until they go to pointe and throughout their dance careers by men wear out from use, but also at a rate that depends in part on the dancer's metabolism and how much he or she sweats. It depends, too, partly on the kind of floor the dancer is working on. A smooth-surfaced floor is easier on shoes. Working correctly also adds life to ballet slippers. If you're not scuffing your feet on the floor when you move and are working properly, and if you are not digging into the floor to point your toe and are working in to the center of the foot, the shoes should last longer.

If you find that you are getting a hole under the big toe of your slippers, it may be due to a rough floor, but it may indicate that you are putting too much pressure on the toe and not using the other four toes when you dance. Holes in the toe area may also indicate that you are overextending the slide along the floor when you move.

Actually, you can tell quite a lot about the way you're working from looking at your ballet slippers. Look at the bottoms, for example. The dirt picked up from the floor should be an even, dark impression, like the imprint of toes, ball, and heel with raised arch that you make when you walk on sand or make an ink impression of the bare foot. If the bottoms of the shoes are darkened only along the outside of the sole from toe to heel, you're not working on the whole foot as you should be, but are probably working too much on the outside of your foot and leaning heavily to your heels. The end result of this habit, if not corrected, may be shin splints (which we talk about in Chapter 8), as well as shoes that wear out more quickly than they should.

Because ballet slippers are expensive and do wear out eventually no matter what kind of care you take of them, I often see students wearing the same pair for a long, long time, making emergency repairs to help them last just a little longer. When big toes wear out, they use masking tape or adhesive tape to hold the shoe together, they patch and tape and sew to hold off the inevitable. This kind of emergency repair may help you get through a class in the shoes, but it isn't permanent, and wearing the shoes may be an uncomfortable experience. Wearing a slipper that's being held together with makeshift repairs may, more importantly, cause the dancer to trip in the midst of a jump or a difficult combination, and he or she may end up with an injury that's far more expensive in terms of medical treatment and time lost from dancing than a new pair of ballet slippers.

All dancers have to learn to sew the elastics that hold the slipper on the foot. Although most dancers think they know how, I often see students who should know better doing it incorrectly.

The elastics across the arch should not be too confining. When you go up on half pointe, you should feel that the slipper is secure without the sensation that the elastic is cutting into the foot and cutting off circulation, or not allowing you to bend the arch easily to reach half pointe. The heel of the slipper should be held securely, but again, not constricted (too tight or too loose). You had better make sure the shoes themselves are the right size for you.

When you are standing flat on your feet, the elastics should just fit comfortably across your foot. Don't use too short a piece of elastic, so that it's stretched even when you are at rest, or it will cut into the foot. Constant pressure and rubbing from the elastics at rest and dancing may cause a callus in the area.

To sew elastics properly, first measure the length of the elastic from one side of the shoe to the other across the foot, and allow a little extra elastic (very little) for the sewing. Fold the heel of the slipper inward toward the inside of the shoe. Two diagonal folds will be formed, one on each side of the slipper. Sew the elastic to the inside of the binding at these two points.

Use heavy enough thread so that the stretch of the elastic won't tear out the stitches, and use three-quarter-inch or half-inch elastic. Narrower widths will cut into the foot even if the elastic is the right length.

If you don't do it right the first time, do it over again.

When you finish class, don't just toss your damp slippers into your practice bag. The perspiration-soaked leather will dry out and crack, and the shape of the shoe will be lost. Instead, fold the heel of the slipper into the toe, and then stretch the toe repeatedly for a while to keep its shape. Then, as soon as you can, put the slippers in a place where air circulates to dry them out. You'll find that if you do this regularly, your ballet slippers stand a good chance of lasting longer.

About Pointe Shoes

The dancer who is making the transition from slippers to pointe shoes will probably first be taking fifteen minutes or so of pointe work after ballet class to gain strength and familiarize herself with the more supportive shoe and different balance of the body before taking a regular pointe technique class. I sometimes also recommend that a developing dancer wear old toe shoes for center work. The worn shoes can't support her on pointe, but the structure of the shoe is more confining than a ballet slipper, and the feel on the foot is closer to what she will be experiencing on pointe. Some more experienced dancers take a ballet barre and wear pointe shoes for center work, doing as much as they can through their pointes. This serves as additional preparation for pointe technique class and helps to build strength, which can be tested by *allegro* movements, how quickly the ankles work, the strength of the foot when landing from a jump, and the speed of the ankles when doing a *relevé* to full pointe.

The pattern of wear on the bottom of toe shoes can, as in the case of ballet slippers, give you an indication of the way you are working. If you are not picking up dirt evenly around the whole bottom of the shoe, but only on the outside or inside edge, or toward the heel, you are not working on the entire foot as you should be, and are rolling in or out. Either of these can have an effect on your technique and can stress muscles and tendons, causing chronic conditions such as shin splints or problems with the Achilles tendon.

Toe shoes are even more expensive than ballet slippers, and there is a lot to know about caring for them to make them last and keep in shape so that you can dance well in them. Much of what I will mention here has been picked up simply by listening to other dancers; they are tricks of the trade that have been useful to me and other dancers I know. Keep your ears open—you never know when one of your fellow dancers will come up with a solution to a problem.

SEWING RIBBONS

Sewing ribbons on toe shoes goes back to the way elastics are sewn for ballet slippers. Fold in the heel toward the inner sole, and at the diagonal creases that form on each side of the shoe or just in front (depending on your arch), sew the ribbons to the inside of the binding. Cut the ribbons a bit long so you will be able to reuse them on new shoes.

The satin-faced ribbon used for toe shoes (seven-eighths-inch or three-quarter-inch) is strong, with a certain amount of give to it so that it won't tear or split when it's tied and you are dancing. Ribbon too can be expensive, and it's usually more economical to buy it by the roll. Since ribbons last longer than the shoes, they can be taken off the worn shoe, washed, and resewn on a new pair. The outside ribbon is generally longer than the inside one, so be sure to resew them on the correct sides of the shoe. Don't cut the ribbons too short to save a few inches. Instead, sew them on with a double fold of ribbon for extra life. They have to be long enough so that when you tie them, you will have enough ribbon to make a double slip knot that you tuck underneath the ribbon around the ankle (but never tuck a knot under on the back of the foot, where it can create a callus or pressure on the ankle tendon).

Once when I was a young dancer working in the corps de ballet at the Radio City Music Hall, I went onstage with ribbons that were too short. I tied them, tucked the ends and knot in, wetting them so the ribbon seemed to stick, and went onstage. In the middle of a quick *allegro* movement, my ribbons just slipped out of the knot, and there I was in the middle of a performance, with dangling ribbons and terror in my heart. It never happened to me again.

Sewing the ends of tied ribbons if they are a little too short for a firm knot seems like a perfect emergency solution, but remember that this does not allow the ribbon to stretch even slightly as you dance, and without that give, the ribbon may split from the shoe in the middle of a performance (another small disaster that I once experienced, but *only* once!). Sometimes, if you sew the ribbons before a performance that includes a quick change in the middle, and you discover the shoes have worn out, there are two minutes for the costume change and no minutes to change shoes and the sewn ribbons, you may have a problem. Try to exist without sewing your ribbons; cut them long enough in the first place, and learn to tie knots that will hold.

Inside the binding that finishes off the edge of the shoe is a cord a little thicker than string which serves to keep the shape of shoes as they stretch with wearing. If you have to pull the cord too tight when you first buy the shoe to keep it on your foot, you have a shoe that doesn't fit properly. It is only after the shoe has been worn and has stretched somewhat that you pull the cord tighter to hold the shape. Instead of making a bow at the ends of the cord where it comes from the binding at the top of the foot, tie a knot and reverse it, so it doesn't slip. I never tuck the ends of the cord into the shoe, as this can cause a callus. Rather, I snip the ends and sew them to the binding so the shoe has a finished line.

BREAKING IN SHOES

The best way to break in toe shoes (especially if you plan to wear them onstage) is to allow time to break them in during class or backstage warmup, or as part of a rehearsal. As you go through the proper exercises of balance, the articulation of the ankle, and the balance of the foot through the whole body, the shoes will be broken in and ready for dancing. You can also manipulate them gently by hand to help break them in, especially if you manipulate the back part of the sole.

Don't resort to sticking shoes in a door to crack them or dousing them with alcohol. The alcohol trick does stretch shoes and break them in, but the result is ruined shoes. The glue in the canvas support on the inside of the shoe is diluted by the alcohol, the box becomes misshapen, and the shoe cannot be reconstructed. I won't deny, however, that alcohol is a useful emergency measure (rather than an acceptable common practice). Suppose, for example, you have broken in your shoes, but you have been overworking and your feet are swollen. No remedy seems to take away the swelling, and you have to dance in those shoes. Then you might use alcohol to stretch the shoes—but be aware that the shoe is likely to be ruined. The alcohol should be directed to the satin so the heel will stretch to fit the foot.

While performing, I always had a number of shoes broken in and ready, since preparation seems to me to be extremely important for a dancer, especially in performing with a company or doing concert work. Pointe shoes seem to have a life of their own, incidentally, and each different ballet has an effect on the life of the shoe. The performer has to be ready for anything and everything.

Dancers have devised all sorts of ways to make sure their shoes aren't loose during a performance. Sometimes backstage at theaters there's a water bucket so that dancers can dip their heels in water before dancing to shrink the shoe slightly. This works (if you're careful not to get the shoes too wet), but it is also dangerous. The floor, especially a surface like linoleum, becomes slippery when wet, and more slippery still if the water mixes with resin.

One method that works well for keeping the heels secure is a home remedy. Place a dab of ordinary white glue no larger than a dime on the inside of the shoe at the sides of the heel (not on the back of the heel). When you put on the shoes, the glue will catch on your tights and the heel will hold securely when you dance. The glue washes off the tights easily. If glue builds up on the shoe, don't try to wash it; just dip the heel in water, let the excess water drip off, and put on the shoe. The built-up glue will dissolve slightly with this treatment and again catch to the tights. Washing off glue by soaking in water will damage the shoe and shrink it.

CARE OF SHOES

Perspiration from dancing can be very hard on pointe shoes, as are humidity and warm temperatures. Dampness of any kind softens the point that is directly on the floor, and the box gets spongy and loses its shape. Dancers have found a number of ways to prevent this from happening. Some use a glob of spirit gum (the kind used for putting on false mustaches, which you can get at theatrical stores), or a commercial product like Fabulon. If you do this, make sure it is completely dry before you work in the shoes; otherwise it might cause irritation or blisters. I used to use heavy brown paper from the market to absorb perspiration and protect the box. I would cut a piece about three or four inches by two and a half inches and wrap it around my toes, folding it over the way you would fold wrapping paper on the end of a package. Some dancers use paper towels, others lamb's wool —anything to protect the shoes, as long as it's not too bulky.

If you feel that the arch or sole of the shoe has gotten too soft, you can use Fabulon on the *outside* of the sole for stiffness. (Don't use this on the inside or the tips, however.) Some dancers use clear acrylic floor wax to stiffen shoes. This is more or less an emergency measure, since you shouldn't be buying shoes that are too soft to begin with. No matter how strong your feet are, when you are fatigued you can damage your Achilles tendon in too-soft shoes, the sense of balance changes, and the thighs are overworked. With normal placement on pointe altered, your dancing will suffer, and while you may think you are getting stronger, all you are actually doing is changing your balance. Overworking the thighs and ankles can cause tendonitis to develop.

After you have finished working in pointe shoes, you must get the moisture out of them. Put them on a window sill or someplace where the air circulates around them, so that they will dry. When you do this, in order to keep the shape, fold the heel into the inside sole, fold the folds over each other, and wrap the ribbons around the shoes to keep the heel in shape. Tuck the ends of the ribbon under the fold, and then use your hand to stretch the front part of the box.

Someone is always coming up with another idea for the care of pointe shoes. Some dancers turn the oven to high, and when it's heated, turn it off and put their damp toe shoes in, unfolded, to dry out. One day I opened the refrigerator to put away a roast and discovered a pair of toe shoes on a shelf with their ribbons dangling into a pot of soup. My daughter had discovered that putting her shoes into the refrigerator to dry made them last two days longer. (But don't use either oven or refrigerator if the shoes have been treated with anything like Fabulon—and inform your family that the shoes in the refrigerator are there intentionally, and not because you've been under so much pressure you can't remember where you're putting your shoes!)

Again, pay attention to what other dancers have discovered to be useful home remedies. Remember, though, that strong chemical products should be used with care so they don't damage the materials of the shoe or react somehow with the body.

OTHER SHOE HINTS

Lamb's wool is a great boon to dancers, and can solve various problems. For toe shoes, if you have toes that slope on a diagonal, you may want to use a little lamb's wool to fill in the point of the shoe (this doesn't mean you don't make an effort to get a shoe with a box as close to your foot conformation as possible, however). On the other hand, I have known a lot of dancers who never wear anything in their shoes, and as a result their toes get tougher, which is good. Sometimes you might have to use a bit of lamb's wool between two toes when foam rubber pads won't do, but this is something you learn by experience.

Be wary of broken shanks; for the most part, the shoe is no longer usable if this happens. Once I performed in shoes that were so comfortable—but the shanks were broken, and I sprained the under part of my arch as a result. I was out of action for ten days, and painfully so, with another month required to revitalize the area.

Injuries caused by carelessness about shoes aren't necessary. If you are a performer, you have to keep in mind that you have not only inconvenienced yourself by being unable to dance, but you have also betrayed something of your responsibility to the company, which expects you to be able to dance as required. For the student, injuries mean setbacks in progress. There is no reason why a dancer cannot take the responsibility for finding out what is right for him or her. Experience teaches a great deal, but above all you have to have a willingness to ask questions of anyone who might be able to point you in the right direction.

What Dancers Wear

Some dance studios and many of the institutional schools of dance have strict dress requirements based on class levels—a certain color of leotard, a certain color of tights, depending on the class. Young people tend to rebel at such conformity, especially when introduced to it after being in classes where they could wear what they chose.

If you find yourself studying at a school with dress requirements, don't waste your mental, emotional, and physical energy on criticizing them; uniformity of dress in class does not deny the individuality of the dancer. Your individuality is expressed through movement. Ballet is, in a sense, a matter of conforming to strict rules of movement and position, yet this in itself sets the dancer free to express himself or herself creatively within the rules.

Another aspect of uniform dress, especially in the institutional schools, is the matter of the school's image. One student at the School of American Ballet commented that she didn't mind the dress requirements; the different combinations of leotards and tights as students go on to higher-level classes mark progress, and she noted too that observers at the classes can better judge what individual dancers are doing if they aren't distracted by many different kinds of practice clothes.

For open classes, there are generally no dress requirements. I never tell my students what to wear, and they are free to dress as they please. Yet over a period of time they gradually simplify their practice clothes, with more and more conformity in style within the classes.

Even if you are free to wear whatever you want to class, certain guidelines are important.

A flash of red in class, for example, can be distracting to you, the teacher, and the rest of the class. Stripes are distracting. Black, pink, and white leotards and tights are the most suitable. (If you don't look well in light colors, check your weight.) Second, the combination of properly fitting tights and leotard is a standard for dancers and for a very good reason: the person teaching the dancer, and the dancer himself or herself, can see how the body looks without encumbrances or constrictions.

The clothes a dancer wears must never hide the lines of the body and in the process perhaps cover up deficiencies that need to be corrected. If the dancer is wearing heavy leg warmers, sweat pants, and a bulky shirt, the teacher can't see what needs correction, and you can't see how you look when you move. Dancers do wear heavy socks in a cold climate, but when it's warm enough, there's no reason to. A heavy sweater doesn't allow the articulation of the arms to be seen, and this relates to the development of the back. If the teacher doesn't see the deficiency, you stand no chance of having him or her correct a weakness that could become chronic.

Sweat pants, rubber pants, and the like don't help you lose weight permanently; the weight loss is only temporary. If you need to keep your legs warm, wear wool tights or something that clings to the line of the leg. Skirts hide the shape of the hips over your thighs, and if you work incorrectly for a long time in this area, a distortion of balance results because no one has been able to see the hip in the line of the leg from the waist. You may have a "comfortable" balance to your body, but you will not have a proper line from your toes to your head.

At one class being given by Mr. Balanchine, a dancer showed up in rubber pants from ankle to waist, with another rubber garment from waist to neck and over her arms, and a heavy scarf around her throat and heavy socks around her ankles.

"Are you unwell?" Mr. Balanchine asked her.

"Not at all," she said. "I'm feeling fine."

"Are you sure you don't have a cold?"

"No. I feel wonderful."

"Then why are you wearing all these clothes?" he asked.

The dancer hesitated for a moment, and then said, "Because I don't like looking at myself."

If you seem to be wearing a lot of excess clothes and socks and the like to dance, ask yourself why. Have they become coverups and crutches for defects that need work to correct? Do you not like looking at yourself? And if not, why? There has to be something wrong with what you are doing if you can't face a reflection of yourself with clean, uncluttered lines, and if you are covering up, you know, at least unconsciously, what it is.

The Dancer's Hair

Long hair is practically the mark of a young woman dancer. For the professional, of course, it's almost a necessity, since different ballets require different hair styles, and the long hair provides flexibility, lending itself to the many shapes that are part of the dancer's adornment onstage.

Most student dancers keep their hair long, and if you're in line for a chance to perform, this is probably wise. One of my students debated cutting her long hair for quite a while, and of course, the day after she had it cut, she got a job in the ballet with a major opera company, where long hair was needed. She went off on a search for an appropriate wig—but wigs are not really a satisfactory alternative.

Whether a young woman's hair is short, medium length, or long, the only strict requirement is that it not be a distraction, and that it not cover up the shape of the head and the line of head and neck. The teacher wants to help you develop a clean line from head to foot; hair that flies off in all directions, a pony tail that hits you in the eye when

The do's and don'ts of dress.

you do pirouettes, pins that fall out when you move are all unwanted and unnecessary distractions.

Ideally, your hair should be neat and under control so that the shape of the head is constant. When you look at yourself in the mirror, you should have a full, clean picture of yourself. Use the mirror to correct yourself—use it objectively as a part of the teacher's instruction, and not as a chance to admire yourself.

Young men should keep their hair at a length that won't interfere with dancing or the look of the head. One young man in class had long, heavy, straight hair, and he tended to perspire quite a bit as well. As a result, he would have trouble spotting in doing pirouettes because his hair would hit him in the face, although at first he couldn't figure out what was wrong. With shorter hair, his turns got better.

Jewelry

Dancers should not wear lethal jewelry when they take class—protruding rings, long chains, heavy bracelets, anything that might hit another dancer. Wear jewelry that is close to the skin if you must wear jewelry at all.

Don't bring expensive watches, valuable rings, and so forth to class; these are things you will take off at the washstand and forget. Invariably, they are gone when you come back to look for them. If for some reason you must bring valuables to class, don't leave them in the dressing room, but with the person at the desk.

What to Carry in Your Dance Bag

The dance bag is sort of a dancer's home-away-from-home, and it should contain items for every need and for most emergencies. I'd suggest that you make most items a permanent part of your equipment in the bag, rather than things you take out and also use at home. It is worth investing in two of everything. Sample size products sold at drugstores are handy, since they don't take up a lot of room in the bag, and they're inexpensive. Almost everything listed is useful for both men and women, and don't forget to keep your ears open for other suggestions you may hear around the studio.

CLOTHES AND SHOES

Extra ballet and/or pointe shoes
Extra tights, leotards
Sweater
Leg warmers
Underwear
For men, extra dance belt, suspenders/tight holders

SEWING KIT

Needles
Thread (two kinds: regular and heavy)
Scissors (small folding scissors are readily available)
Safety pins
Extra elastic, ribbons, waist elastic

FIRST AID

Band-Aids
Tincture of Merthiolate
Medicated foot powder
Alcohol
Aspirin
Vitamins
For women, extra tampons, and so on

APPEARANCE AND HYGIENE

Hairnet
Pins and clips
Comb and brush
Hair spray

For men, head band
Deodorant
Toothpaste and toothbrush
Soap
Towels
Makeup

EXTRAS

Folding drinking cup (many studios don't have paper cups)
Snacks—granola bars, fruit, fruit juice
Notebook for corrections
Pencil
Extra change (enough to get you home if you lose your purse or wallet)
Extra house keys (for the same reason)

Remember to have a bag that zips closed, and this also applies to purses. Most studios make provision for keeping bags and purses under someone's eye while class is going on. Take advantage of this, especially if you have something you can't afford to lose.

PART III
The Dancer's Body

6

HEALTH AND THE DANCER

The dancer's body is the only instrument he or she has. We use it to perform the steps that produce the movement that make pictures in space and time; these, in turn, express and evoke emotion for and from an audience. It's a House-that-Jack-built relationship between the parts that ends with dance—but begins with the instrument. It's the only body we have; it's irreplaceable. No second chances, no spare parts.

Just as you can't be careless when it comes to the learning of technique and must always be questioning what you are doing and what you are being taught, so you can't be indifferent about how you treat your body, how it works, what it looks like. Discovery in dance doesn't have to do just with challenging your abilities or establishing your artistry in dance. It has to do also with finding out *everything* that has a bearing on dance. This translates into very practical considerations about keeping healthy, preventing injuries, and healing them when they do occur.

There is really no excuse for being careless about your health and physical well-being. It is part of the preparation to dance that I believe is so important, as much as having your shoes broken in when they're needed and the right equipment in your dance bag. I know from my own experience and the experiences of students that the pressures of living and dancing, of perhaps going to school or working at a job, of dealing with personal relationships, and of having to grow up quickly with a lot of responsibility for yourself take precedence over matters like eating right and taking time to rest.

Diet and Nutrition for Dancers

Like athletes, dancers are always in training, but many young dancers at all levels of study forget this. While a good teacher can help the young dancer in many ways that make his or her body a more perfect instrument, the responsibility for giving the body the proper care, the right food, and enough rest belongs to the dancer.

You have to be aware that there is always bad advice floating around. Fads about diet abound, and sometimes it seems easier to forget the whole thing, and eat and sleep and work and play any way at all, and never mind the consequences.

Let me say this: Although I am not a nutritionist, I have always been a listener and a learner. I've made it a point to find out what is good for me and what isn't. It's not difficult to do, and the most important aspect is a good share of common sense.

To make what has to be an obvious and fundamental point: The food you eat is the fuel for the instrument. It's part of your training and the awareness that you're trying to achieve something with it, whether it is onstage with a major ballet company in New York City, dancing with a modern company or with a regional ballet, doing a dance demonstration, or taking a good ballet class where you feel strong and accomplish what the teacher asks of you.

It seems logical, then, that anyone who wants to be in good physical condition to dance must pay attention to the food he or she eats. This is *not* a fad. You must learn what is good for you and why, and what is not, as well as the special nutritional and supplementary needs of a physically active person who uses up a lot of energy day after day. And then you have to make that knowledge part of your life. You make time for meals, and proper ones at that. You take enough time to relax and let your body renew itself. You don't deprive yourself of the nutritional fuel you need in the constant (and often, I think, unnecessary) concern for losing weight that is practically a way of life for young dancers.

Fad diets don't work, either for weight loss or to supply a dancer's nutritional needs. A balanced diet is needed: protein, fruits and vegetables, grains, dairy products, with the necessary vitamins and minerals. A basic nutrition book can tell you this, and if you are unaware of the established nutritional requirements for an active young person, you should find out what they are. A good multivitamin supplement every day is helpful, and these are readily available at drugstores and health food stores. High dosages of particular vitamins, unless they have been specifically recommended by a physician, are very questionable. Some vitamins taken in excess (vitamins A and D, for example) can have dangerous side effects; in the case of other vitamins, the body can only use a given amount daily, and any extra taken just means wasted money. Again, there are any number of authoritative books available that talk about the vitamin and mineral needs of normal, healthy young people.

Given the pressures of a schedule that differs from that of nondancing family members or requires living in a strange city where you have do your own shopping, it's admittedly hard to incorporate a proper diet in all this activity. But a Coke and a hamburger from a fast-food restaurant grabbed on the run, or a slice of pizza or a hotdog, day after day, can't carry you through classes. A heavy dose of sugar from soft drinks or chocolate and the rush of energy from them can't replace a proper diet. A proper diet also doesn't mean starving yourself—whether to lose weight or just to save time.

You must, first of all, have breakfast. There are arguments for and against a substantial breakfast, but I believe a dancer in training needs this meal. To have a *good* breakfast, both nutritionally and for the energy it gives you, you have to get up early enough to be able to eat it and digest it before your nine or ten o'clock class begins. Otherwise, you'll feel bloated and sluggish. A bowl of hot oatmeal or another grain cereal can give you the kind of energy you're going to need. If you like to eat bread, it should be a natural grain product (the less treated, the less laced with preservatives, the better, for anything you eat). Maybe you like eggs occasionally, or something unconventional early in the morning (some people don't like the usual breakfast foods; there's no rule that says you can't have soup, for example, if that's what appeals to you). What you shouldn't do is start the day with coffee and a doughnut and expect to get through a dance class at the top of your energy level.

Sometimes when you've been working hard all morning, you do need a pickup; make it a point to tuck a granola bar, fresh or dried fruit, sunflower seeds, or a small can of fruit juice in your dance bag, so you won't be tempted with candies or soft drinks that are loaded with sugar.

I myself seldom eat more than yogurt or something equally light during the day, since I've learned that eating slows me up. Others may have a different metabolism and require a more substantial daytime meal. It's a question of knowing yourself and the needs of your body and especially the digestive system. Most dancers will probably work more effectively if they eat lightly during the day: yogurt, wheat germ, salads, fruit. If you have had a proper breakfast you won't need more, and your energy level will remain high. No going hungry though, which can make you extremely tense and nervous. I've seen dancers become depressed and irritable, and even fall into crying jags, when they've allowed the level of blood sugar to drop through not eating (usually because they're trying to lose weight or they think they're "too busy" to eat). This is not the way to train productively; you will not be taking instruction with a proper attitude, and you're likely to become careless—a sure way to injure yourself.

A good dinner in the evening is important. It doesn't have to be a large meal (if you *are* trying to lose weight, cutting down on portions and thus calories is the most effective kind of diet). It should include the protein you need, in the form of meat, fish, poultry, or legumes; vegetables; and salad. There's nothing wrong in including some carbohydrates in the form of potatoes (but *not* French fries), rice, or pasta. The natural sugar in fruits or grain products is better for you than the refined sugars found in sweet desserts. Although frozen convenience foods seem like a boon to busy people, they are an expensive luxury, and also are not good choices to form the basis of your diet. The fewer processed foods you eat, the better. Especially if you're on your own with a limited budget, you're far better off financially and nutritionally broiling some hamburger or chicken and making a big salad than resorting regularly to the packaged meals in the frozen food department of the supermarket.

Carbohydrates feed and soothe tired muscles; today, many athletes train with higher intakes of carbohydrates than protein. On the day off for rest—which every dancer should take each week—indulge in carbohydrates. Eat the potatoes and spaghetti and rice you've kept away from during your working week to restore muscles fatigued from a full schedule of dancing. If chocolate cake or an ice cream sundae is a forbidden pleasure that you like but deny yourself most of the time, now and then on your day off indulge yourself for at least the psychological boost it will give you. If you're eating a well-balanced diet, your body probably won't crave quantities of sugar, but no one says you can't enjoy yourself now and then—and a hot fudge sundae with all the trimmings can do worlds of good.

Americans, especially young people, seem to grow up accustomed to snacking, and often the most accessible snack food is junk food. Remember to put good snacks, if you need to snack, in your practice bag, and keep away from junk food.

Vitamins and Minerals

Part of good nutrition is making sure that you get adequate amounts of necessary vitamins, minerals, and other dietary elements. If he or she is eating properly and taking a multivitamin supplement, a normal, healthy person shouldn't have any problems. But the special life of the dancer can bring up special conditions you should be aware of.

For example, during the process of dance training, muscle cramps can occur because acidity accumulates in the muscles. Calcium counteracts the acid buildup. You can drink milk, of course, but some people are allergic to milk or don't like it. Or you can ask your doctor about the calcium supplements that are available at health food stores.

Potassium is one of the elements that is readily lost when a dancer perspires (this also occurs in cases of heat prostration, when marathon runners collapse at the wayside). Potassium is essential for the proper functioning of various organs, and a lack of it shows up early in physical fatigue. A very capable and beautiful young woman dancer who came to my studio to study for the summer began complaining that she was suddenly feeling so tired that she could hardly get through a class. I was surprised that someone with her training and experience showed such a lack of energy, especially since dancers usually feel better in summer than winter. The air is warm, the muscles are more pliable, and they don't need to work up energy to make the body react to exercise. I questioned her about her diet, but she seemed to be eating a balanced diet, getting enough rest, drinking enough liquids to replace the water lost through perspiration. I suggested she add a daily multivitamin, and eat more foods rich in potassium: bananas (which are *not* "fattening"), orange juice, tomato juice, even mushrooms. The student took my advice, and a week later felt like her usual self. Various potassium supplements are available at health food stores, but I don't suggest you should be your own doctor and dose yourself heavily with this or any kind of dietary supplement. A physician can guide you in this. But I do suggest that you understand what might be needed and try to eat the foods that will supply minerals like potassium that can make a real difference to your dancing life.

All of what I've been saying is actually basic knowledge and common sense. When a dancer is deeply involved in training and constantly on the move, it's easy to forget what's best. The young dancer has to remember that he or she is still growing physically, and the body is changing and developing through the teens and into the twenties. The teen-age years are no time to ignore the requirements of good nutrition; it's one of the responsibilities of being a dancer. Athletes are often under the eyes of their coaches, who make sure they're eating and sleeping right. Dancers have similar physical requirements, but seldom have the same guidance; they have to do it themselves.

Nutrition is as important to a dancer as getting toe shoes that fit and the right tights and leotard. Every dancer must be aware of that simple fact. The other key word is moderation: overdo nothing; take your nutritional pleasures in moderation.

Losing Weight and "Getting Thinner"

The idea that "thinner is better" is common to a lot of people, dancers and nondancers alike. However, being the "right" weight and being thinner are not necessarily the same things.

For the dancer in training, I wonder how much is a genuine need to get slimmer and how much is a feeling of frustration about the work. Is the dancer asking, in effect, "Why am I not satisfied and happy with myself when I dance?" The easy answer is, if I lose weight (or change the color of my hair or buy new clothes or make some other change), I won't be the person I'm unhappy with.

Perhaps, instead of worrying about losing weight, the dancer should be asking: "What is really frustrating me about my work—a few extra pounds, or something else—my technique, my attitude, my health?"

One student who was working well had lots of energy, and was slim (the "right" weight). But she wasn't happy with herself; in fact, she was constantly unhappy and frustrated. Someone she relied on for advice suggested she "get thinner," but the effort didn't produce the desired results. She became more frustrated and discontented. In fact, there was nothing wrong with this dancer except fatigue, but she had allowed frustration to lead her to grasp at excuses for herself and too-easy answers: getting thinner would solve all her problems.

Don't allow frustration to cloud your intelligence and your understanding of your needs as a dancer.

One source of frustration about weight has to do with the misguided view that by getting much thinner, a dancer will be more appealing to the artistic directors of some ballet companies; that by some magic, losing weight will alter the unalterable, the particular bone and muscle build he or she was born with; that being thinner will automatically make a person a better dancer.

None of this is true. Your technique, your ability to move in space and time, and the way you use the body you were born with and have trained for years determine your success as a dancer, not your ability to lose pounds.

Young dancers often fail to realize that dancers in their teens are generally expected to carry a bit more weight than they will a few years later, because they need it for growth and energy. Another point is that dieting can be physically taxing and mentally depressing. Starvation diets, too often undertaken by young dancers, can do tremendous damage.

Of course, slimness is part of being a dancer; dancers do have to monitor their weight, and thinness, besides its visual aspect, has other implications for dancers. There is some proof, according to Dr. L. M. Vincent, writing in *Competing with the Sylph*, that the irregular menstrual cycles of many woman dancers may be attributed in part to the low amounts of body fat in the active dancer's body. "We may comfortably accept at least one straightforward, causal relationship," he says, "namely, 'thinness'—in and of itself or along with the 'stress' of dancing—may be responsible for both the delay in the onset of menstruation as well as the lack of maintenance of a regular menstrual cycle."

But being thin can become a dangerous obsession; it can lead the dancer to excess in an area where moderation should be the keynote. The extreme that can be reached is anorexia nervosa, which often starts with a refusal to eat in order to get thinner and develops into a physical and psychological condition characterized by a total aversion to food. It is, in fact, a serious illness, and sufferers don't look "thin"; they look sick and emaciated. To reverse the condition not only does the sufferer have to deal with the physical effects, but she must overcome the mental problems. Most anorexic people are girls in their early and mid-teens—just the time when dancers are really getting into training and worrying about their weight—although it can occur in later years as well. I do not suggest any form of starvation, both for what it can do to weaken the dancer physically even over short periods of time, and certainly for what it can become in terms of a medical problem if carried to the extreme of anorexia.

Yet there are occasions when it is advisable to lose some weight. You can notice a weight buildup when you watch yourself dance in a mirror; your teacher might see that you've gained some unneeded weight. How do you lose it?

Again, take no extreme measures of any kind. And remember that diets and medication and rubber pants that eliminate water and cause a temporary weight loss don't mean that you are actually getting thinner. Instead, look at what you're eating. Too many Cokes between classes? Potato chips? (Maybe your body craves salt; try eating bacon or the like occasionally.) Too many sandwiches grabbed on the run, thick bread, heavy with mayonnaise? If you pay attention, you can tell quickly enough if you're indulging in empty, weight-producing calories, and then cut them out.

You want to be still thinner? Try eating smaller quantities. That's the ideal diet. Don't believe in any magic diet of a single food or a bizarre combination of foods. It doesn't exist, and if you try one, you may see a quick weight loss (often largely water) that doesn't last. Check with your friends who've tried such diets; chances are high that the weight is back in a few weeks.

I can't emphasize enough that sensible eating must take precedence over the possible loss of a few pounds under stringent and damaging conditions. The body must have fuel to operate. The only way to obtain that fuel is through food.

If you decide to try a diet that's more specialized than simply eating a little less and cutting out the Twinkies, you'd be well advised to talk to your doctor first. If, in the end, you don't take my advice and go on some diet on your own, limit yourself to a week or ten days of it. And when it comes to losing weight, don't expect miracles.

Rest and Relaxation

If food is the fuel for a dancer's body, rest is the restorer. If you're working four, five, or six hours a day, six days a week, you need plenty of sleep and periods of rest—eight hours of sleep a night or more, and rest between classes. Young people tend to need more sleep than older people in any case. And if you're working hard, you have to take off one day every week, just for rest.

Again, I'm speaking of logic and common sense. Dedicated people sometimes see themselves as supermen and superwomen, and forget all about common sense. The day off itself means that you have a chance to be less the super person and more like the rest of the world. It's a chance to socialize outside of dance circles, to let your mind as well as your body relax and revitalize itself.

A student who works hard, is happy about what he or she is doing, and enjoys the pressures of taking difficult classes suddenly explodes in unexpected anger or has a crying jag because of a chance remark by the teacher or another student. Is it really what somebody said or the way the class went that morning? Or is it that the dancer's mind and body are exhausted? Often it's the latter. You need rest, sleep, detachment from what you've been doing. The young dancer, pressing to learn and succeed, has to be aware of those fatigue signals, both of mind and muscle. You can't press yourself beyond endurance and expect to work well in class day after day. (This is especially true if you're employed or going to school as well as studying dance.) For one thing, if you're tired, you're more accident prone. Oddly enough, when there's fatigue, you often feel you're working your best because muscle memory somehow carries you through automatically, and that's when you sprain your ankle, or hurt a knee by stretching a ligament. The automatic physical response doesn't seem to be related to a mental response. (Remember, too, that when you've been resting an injury for a week or so, and come back feeling great, you have to work back to the point where you were when you were injured. *Slowly* is the key word.)

Mental fatigue can be corrected only by sleep, but "catching up" on sleep is an emergency measure. You're far better off getting regular, sufficient sleep and rest.

Along with regular sleep, a dancer has to take time for periods of rest during the day, between classes or between class and the time you have to be at work, at school, or doing homework (even more so if you are working extra hard academically for early graduation). Ideally, you should be able to go home between classes and relax. The best kind of rest for a dancer is taking a lukewarm bath for half an hour. One student of mine said, "I run home, take a half-hour nap, and feel terrific!" Both are as restoring to your mind and body as three hours of sleep.

If you can't manage to get home, try to relax somewhere with a book. Go to the library or a park. In New York, students have the opportunity to go to the Lincoln Center Library of the Performing Arts, where they can make appointments to see ballet films.

When I was a young dancer starting out with the New York City Ballet, I lived with my sister in New Jersey. It wasn't possible to go home during breaks in training and rehearsing to rest, and I also had long days, getting on a bus to Manhattan at eight in the morning, often not getting home until nine or ten at night. Being a newcomer, I had few acquaintances in the city to distract me, so I sometimes used to turn to the cheapest movie I could find and sit there quietly for a couple of hours. Then I returned to class or rehearsal refreshed and relaxed. Cheap movies aren't so easy to find nowadays (and in New York, not ones that are also safe), but movies now and then still provide the kind of detachment from work that a dancer needs.

Relaxation and rest from dancing don't mean running around shopping or doing chores between classes. It also doesn't mean getting together with friends and other dancers to rehash the class and career plans or dance anxieties. Such conversations aren't necessarily a relaxing exchange of ideas and information, but a way for all concerned to verbalize their worries and use their companions to work through them. See your friends, of course, but don't put yourself in situations where the stresses you're trying to get away from for an hour or two are talked over and the anxieties are fed by the people you're with.

There's another point about rest from dancing that young dancers sometimes overlook, but which I've become especially aware of through my teaching. A number of my students, and certainly young people all across the country, are still in school and have academic responsibilities, particularly as the school year ends and the time for term papers and exams arrives. However important dancing is, this is a time when they must focus their energies on school work. If they allow a conflict to develop, they will perform well in neither situation, the drain on their energy and concentration is doubled, and the frustration of not measuring up is damaging to their images of themselves as dancers and as people.

Learn to understand about priorities. You can, for example, take part of a class to keep in condition, and concentrate your mental and physical energy on what is really more important at the moment. Usually these situations last not much longer than a few days or a week. You will not be falling far behind in dance, and you will be fulfilling one of your many responsibilities. If you don't handle such situations properly, those few days of confusion may mean a month of recuperation to regain lost strength and concentration.

Times of stress or crisis come to all of us: an illness in the family, a personal relationship that's difficult to deal with, responsibilities to face that have nothing to do with dancing. I've said a dancer has to learn to step into a cocoon when he or she steps into the classroom and to forget the push and pull of the outside world. You can't, however, insulate yourself from all other priorities; you have to be flexible enough to rearrange them, without detriment to dance. You don't need to feel guilty if you have to take time away from training. You do have to have the integrity to see the situation for what it is and the patience to work through it, even if it means you don't dance all the hours you wish.

An injury to the dancer often means an enforced time away from dancing. Even if you feel great after only a few days' rest, don't take it upon yourself to disobey doctor's orders and cut short the prescribed recuperation time. Otherwise you can reinjure yourself and end up with a chronic condition no amount of rest will cure. Injuries are one of those priorities. And an injury can mean a reevaluation of your work, just as time out for other priorities can mean a coming to terms with yourself and a reevaluation of yourself as a person.

Exercise for Dancers

If you are a dancer, recreational exercise, such as tennis or jogging or skiing, is something you have to be careful about. The day off every week that I urge every dancer to take really should be for *rest*, for giving back to the muscles what a week of hard work has been taking away.

If you involve yourself in sports on your day off, you're going to continue to use up physical energy instead of restoring it. Moreover, it never seems to fail that a weekend soccer game or touch football or the like leaves the dancer with a broken toe or worse, and a period of enforced time off. To my mind, it simply isn't worth it, however enjoyable that kind of group activity. If your recreational exercise is truly relaxing—swimming, for example—it can be valuable. Social dancing, incidentally, is great recreational exercise. If the activity is a physical or mental drain, you would do well to reconsider what your priorities as a dancer are.

Exercise that's meant to develop and stretch certain muscles is somewhat different. This is, in a sense, part of your dance training. Therapeutic exercise is usually closely supervised by physical therapists or those in charge of schools or sports associations. It still, however, consumes energy that might be better spent in dancing; on the other hand, if you and your teacher feel exercise therapy is important for your development, instead of loading yourself down with an additional hour or two of work a week, you might take it in place of one class. If exercise therapy is correct, it can be constructive.

A Clean Dancer

We all talk about a dancer dancing "cleanly," but I'm speaking now of water and soap and deodorant and good healthy cleanliness. You cannot wear practice clothes more than one day (ideally, if you're working hard, more than one class). They smell, and it's not simply a matter of losing friends and being offensive to other dancers. The perspiration that collects in the clothes is a source of skin problems. The pores open when you dance, the perspiration encourages bacteria to grow, and constant wearing of the same unwashed practice clothes means that the dancer ends up spending money on dermatologists to find out what's wrong with his or her skin.

Similar problems arise when hair is not kept clean all the time. The perspiration and the dirty hair can cause skin problems around the face and neck.

If feet are not kept clean and powdered, the dancer is more susceptible to corns, especially painful and unpleasant ingrown corns. Other foot infections are possible; blisters are likely to become infected.

If you wear clean practice clothes every day and still have skin problems, you would do well to check what you are using to wash the clothes. Some people are sensitive or actually allergic to the ingredients in some detergents. Under normal circumstances they might not be affected by the traces left in the clothes after washing, but the constant contact with perspiration and the open pores may set the conditions for a skin irritation. Change soaps, rinse the clothes thoroughly, and check with your doctor about sensitivity.

The key to good health and the dancer is common sense and moderation, along with taking the responsibility to find out all you can about all the things that concern you, and prepare you to be a dancer.

7

THE DANCER'S FEET

A violinist uses every string on his instrument, the painter needs every color on his palette, a singer sings every note on the scale . . . the list could go on and on. The dancer, too, uses every part of his or her instrument to give form to creativity, and every part has to be kept in good working condition. Everything works together when we dance, yet there's a good reason why dancers put a lot of concern into their feet. The foot extended by a toe shoe is a unique aspect of classical ballet, but the patterns of movement that dancers, classical or modern, make on a stage are possible because they've trained their feet to move their bodies.

It's not surprising that few dancers go through life without ever having any problems with their feet, and even if the collection of bones, muscles, and tendons that make up the feet survive the rigors of dancing without injury, they need constant care to maintain them.

Foot injuries, usually due to carelessness or improper technique, have to be treated correctly, or they can cause problems years later. This happened to me, some twenty years after a broken toe was diagnosed as a sprain and treated as such, with unfortunate results. The operation necessary to correct the lingering but long-unnoticed defect had even more far-reaching implications. After the operation, I felt great after only five days, although I'd been warned to rest the foot longer. But I was walking and feeling good, without realizing that I was actually favoring the healing foot. One day I leaned over to pick something up, and because I'd been favoring the foot and changing my center of balance, my back went out and I was incapacitated for three months. It was stupidity and carelessness that affected not only me but the company, because for that extended period adjustments had to be made in schedules and performances I would have taken part in.

Many foot problems can be avoided if you take care of feet properly, if you understand what causes conditions like blisters and calluses, and if you are aware of how improper technique can lead to injuries. Obviously, you will be better off if you can analyze the reasons for foot problems instead of simply suffering the results, although you have to be aware that it can take as much time to correct a problem as it does to cause it.

Toughening the Skin

Men and women dancers have almost the same kinds of problems with their feet, but the pointe shoe that has evolved over the centuries for women ballet dancers is an added factor in the quest for problem-free dancing feet. Much of what I will discuss relates directly to the dancer on pointe, but the issues I discuss about foot care and injuries apply equally to men in ballet slippers and modern or other types of dancers who may wear no shoes at all or special types of dance shoes. No dancer can move in space without his or her feet, and I don't believe that any form of dance ought to be painful. If your feet hurt when you dance, you are doing something wrong, or there is something wrong with your feet.

I have said that the toe shoe is not a prop for the foot but an extension of the foot, a dressing for the foot the way a glove is a dressing for the hand. When a dancer puts on pointe shoes, she is adding a logical extension to a foot already trained to support the body, adding another dimension to the line of the body—a body (back, legs, thighs, ankles) that is already strong enough to be supported on pointe.

The transition from soft ballet slippers to a boxed toe shoe should not be painful. If the body is strong enough, the dancer experiences a different balance, different pressure, but not pain. The skin of the toes and feet, too, should be sufficiently toughened so that the wearing of pointe shoes is not traumatic. This, of course, is a general rule. Skin is different for each individual. For some people, even working in ballet slippers, where perspiration, pointing, and jumping help toughen skin, does not prepare the foot enough for toe shoes. The fifteen minutes of pointe work after ballet class are helpful in the conditioning process.

Blisters on first wearing pointe shoes are a sign that the skin of the toes hasn't been toughened enough. They may also indicate that the shoe is too big around the toes. Check carefully into the fit, and if you can afford to do so, discard the poorly fitting shoes and get new ones that do fit. In an emergency, you can cut a sock in half and put it into the toe so that you can use the shoes until they wear out.

Toughening comes from working, from constant wearing of toe shoes, so that the perspiration from dancing doesn't cause the skin to remain soft. An important aid in toughening skin is tincture of Merthiolate. Apply it after bathing (it washes off) to the area of your toes where the skin is tender. It will kill any bacteria, and it toughens the tender or irritated areas. Toughening has to do with conditioning and working; the Merthiolate and medicated foot powder help maintain it. Tender skin under toenails can also be protected with Merthiolate and lamb's wool, thinly rolled and slipped under the nail. Don't use so much wool, however, that it takes up too much room in the toe shoe.

Toughened skin is not something that once you have you'll keep forever. Among professionals, the one comment invariably heard after vacations or a couple of weeks away from dancing is, "My toes are so sore!" The skin gets soft again quickly when the dancer isn't working, and there's no way to maintain toughness in the absence of dancing.

Blisters

If you do get a blister on the toes or heel or across the top of the metatarsal where the vamp of the shoe hits the foot, take care of it immediately.

When I was with Ballet Theater and dancing the lead in *Interplay*, which is a rigorous ballet that required me to dance in three of the movements, I wore shoes that were dyed for the performance. Originally, the shoes fit me well, but when they were dyed, the alcohol in the dye shrank them. They were rather tight when I put them on, and I did not have time to break them in properly before the performance. I danced that night, and noticed that the shoe had cut into the heel, causing a small blister. I didn't do more than bathe the area when I got home, and after the next day's performance of *Interplay* in the same shoes, the soreness seemed a bit worse.

Three days later, I had blood poisoning, doctors, antibiotics, and the feeling that I had been very stupid.

The clear fluid that collects in a blister should be drained, either by a doctor or by you, with a well-sterilized needle, and the area treated with an antiseptic, such as Merthiolate, and then protected from further rubbing until healed. If the problem is caused by poorly fitting shoes, blisters will recur until you get the right shoes.

Since perspiration encourages the growth of bacteria, an untreated blister may become infected rapidly. Medicated foot powder is also a must in treating irritated areas.

Occasionally, a blood blister forms; the fluid in the blister is blood instead of clear serum. This should be treated by a doctor or podiatrist. If left untreated, the blood blister may harden and become like a stone bruise, which doesn't go away easily and may cause problems in dancing.

Not every dancer (very few human beings, in fact) has perfectly shaped feet, and toes are seldom of equal length and straight across. You may find that your toes press into the ones next to them. Check first to see that your shoes aren't too small (and "checking" in all these cases means trying on a wide variety of styles until you find the ones that are right for you). If the shoes fit properly, and one toe still presses into the one next to it (usually the second toe pressing into the big toe), you can prevent irritation and possible blisters or corns by using a very thin foam rubber pad between the toes. It won't remove the pressure, of course, but it will protect the skin of the toes. Again, be sure the pad isn't so thick that the foot is cramped and uncomfortable when the shoe is on.

Corns, Calluses, Bunions

Corns and calluses are similar conditions: areas of thickened skin created by constant rubbing. You shouldn't have them, except for conditioning calluses on the tips of your toes. All professional dancers have them here, and are happy to. They can be equated with the calluses a violinist or guitarist gets on the fingers: a mark of the professional. Dancer's calluses on the tips of the toes help protect the toes when dancing on pointe.

Calluses that develop on the heel are a sign of improper technique. They indicate that you are standing on the outside of the foot, and probably not getting to the middle of your toes. The weight is still on the heel, and the pressure causes the callus. Calluses on the metatarsal may indicate that you are wearing shoes that are too tight.

Corns develop on the outside of toes and between them from rubbing and pressure. Again, you must check that your shoes are not too tight or that the box is not too short. When corns become ingrown and hard, they will cause discomfort for the dancer and other problems. Besides relieving any indications of pressure where corns might develop, keep the area dry with foot powder.

Neither corns nor calluses will go away without treatment, even if the pressure is relieved through getting better-fitting shoes. There are commercial products for corn removal, but rather than treating an ingrown corn yourself, or accumulations of white skin between the toes or infections around corns, you would do well to consult a podiatrist. Calluses may be removed by gently rubbing the area with pumice. Don't try to remove either calluses or corns with a razor blade or scissors. You may cut deeply into the skin and provide a site for a serious infection that will be encouraged by the moist environment that occurs when your feet perspire.

A bunion is an inflammation of the small soft tissue sac that lies between the bones and muscles on the outside of the foot, just below the big toe. No dancer should have bunions (unless an arthritic condition exists). Bunions in dancers are caused by the distortion of pressure in that soft tissue area of the big toe. The dancer who has bunions is using the big toe to balance on pointe (which distorts the foot), rather than using all the toes of the foot. She is not going up on her toes through the middle of the metatarsal but favoring the front part of the foot. This not only can cause bunions, but also affects the tendon at the big toe that connects with the arch, resulting in tendonitis of the arch (called "rolling"). You should be dancing evenly on the whole foot, and using the metatarsal to get on pointe—imagine that the foot is a tripod consisting of the big toe, little toe, and heel.

The area where bunions form is a delicate one, the last part of the foot to get strong. A dancer has to listen to what the body is saying. Pain in the area where bunions form is a signal that something is wrong. Steps have to be taken to correct the problem before it becomes chronic. First of all, check your training. Are you avoiding going through the ball of the foot when you go up on pointe? The arch must be in a lifted position at all times, whether on pointe or half pointe, in soft slipper or toe shoe.

Men dancers sometimes get bunions, but not as readily because they don't extend their feet the way women do and don't have the opportunity to put the same incorrect pressure on the inside of the foot. Men can roll, but they can't dance incorrectly for too long. They might have a flexible arch or loose ankle that causes them to roll inward onto that area of the big toe, but when the male dancer gets stronger, his ankles and that part of the foot get stronger, so the bunion problem is less likely. Women without strong ankles, on the other hand, will tend to go inward to that toe when on pointe.

Toenails

In keeping your feet healthy, you shouldn't neglect the toenails. Cut or file them from the outside edge of the nail toward the center so that the nail curves in that direction. Don't allow the middle of the nail to be too long—file it down with an emery board or nail file. Don't cut the nail too short, though, or you will expose soft, tender skin that will be painful and will impede your dancing. If you do happen to cut the nail too short, toughen the exposed skin with tincture of Merthiolate. There are some other commercial products available to cover exposed tender skin, but while they are effective, they can also be painful in the application.

Ingrown toenails, especially in the big toe, can be a problem for the dancer who has a natural tendency to get them. If you have an ingrown nail, use a piece of lamb's wool (in preference to cotton), shredded and then rolled very, very thin and soaked in Merthiolate. Place this under the whole nail so that it protects the toe from the nail on each side. If this trick doesn't help, try splitting the center of the nail in a tiny V and use the rolled-up lamb's wool under the nail. As it grows, the nail will tend to grow together in the center instead of outward into the skin at the outer edge of the nail. A last resort is to clip the nail short at the sides, using very fine scissors. This will probably expose tender skin, so use Merthiolate to protect the area.

Sometimes dancers working on pointe will get bruised toenails; the nail turns black and eventually falls off, and a new nail grows. What happens is the equivalent of hitting a fingernail with a hammer, causing an accumulation of blood under the nail so that it eventually unroots itself and falls off.

Professionals seldom have this problem, unless something heavy does happen to fall on a toe by accident. Young students who aren't quite strong enough to get on pointe sometimes have bruised nails, but a few weeks of work strengthens their toes. Usually the young dancer is curling her toes under in her toe shoes instead of standing straight on the foot with the tip of the toe. Since she is, in effect, gripping or clawing into the toe shoe, the box of the shoe puts pressure on the nail. The pressure can be sufficient to cause the nail bruise.

When a nail falls off, the dancer shouldn't dance on pointe until it has grown back completely. Instead of working with an area of raw skin exposed to perspiration and stress, the dancer would be better off working correctly in ballet slippers to find out what it is she is doing when on pointe that caused the bruised nail. She must also work on getting stronger to correct any deficiency, so that it will not be necessary to curl the toes when on pointe.

Sometimes there is an emergency situation when a student dancer who has lost a nail must dance on pointe in a performance. Since a nail that is about to fall off always has a tender nail growing underneath it, it is possible to dance if the area is well-protected with a foam pad or Band-Aid, but dancing may traumatize the area and delay healing.

Tendonitis

Tendonitis, particularly in the feet and ankles, is a dancer's ailment. It shouldn't be. Properly trained dancers shouldn't have tendonitis. The condition is something of a mystery ailment, although it is common enough among individuals who use their bodies rigorously, and it usually occurs in the part of the body used most strenuously. Baseball pitchers with sore arms, basketball players with sore legs, tennis players with sore elbows, swimmers with sore shoulders, and dancers with sore feet and ankles are very often suffering from tendonitis.

The condition is characterized by an inflammation of the strong fibrous bands of tissue (tendons) that attach the muscles to the bones. The pain is severe when the individual starts to work out, and gradually diminishes. This is what makes tendonitis so much of a problem. If you stop feeling the pain, you continue to work under the conditions that caused it in the first place, inflaming the tendons further. Other indications of tendonitis, besides pain, are problems with pointing the toes, difficulty in moving joints, a locking of the ankle, or a clicking in the ankle when you push off to jump. Constant swelling in the ankle area also suggests tendonitis, as does a joint that doesn't move (the possibility of a hair fracture also exists, and should be checked by a doctor, as I'll discuss later).

The pain of tendonitis when it grips you is something like being hit on the chin or having a sudden toothache. Another type of tendonitis pain is constant, something you get used to, but it's always there. I think of tendonitis in the Achilles area as a murmur that keeps reminding you things aren't right. As I've said, it's possible to work with tendonitis after you've warmed up, but if you stress the area long enough, it will stop working for you. The tendon becomes shorter and shorter with the inflammation, and as it gets thicker, the body takes over to protect itself, and the result is a spasm.

Although most kinds of tendonitis come from repeated stress of an area, it doesn't necessarily take a long time to happen. Even professionals, if they are fatigued or circumstances come together to cause the irritation of a tendon, can temporarily suffer from tendonitis. I was once breaking in shoes for a *pas de deux* that afternoon. The shoes had a high vamp, and my feet were already tired; when I got up on pointe, my foot locked so that I couldn't even remove the shoe, the foot swelled, and I thought I would die from the pain. I had irritated the tendon in the upper arch. It had nothing to do with working incorrectly (although carelessness was a factor). Within three days, I was back to normal with rest that allowed the tendon to heal.

Chronic tendonitis in young dancers, however, is something that should never be. Yet it happens. You have to be alert to the causes and take steps immediately to relieve the stresses that are inflaming the tendons and causing the tendonitis.

Tendonitis in dancers comes from various sources. It may come from working on a very hard floor, usually wood over concrete. If the floor is finished with a material that requires a constant gripping (and not necessarily a slick floor, but linoleum or a gym finish), this can contribute to tendonitis. The actual floor may not be as hard as one with a cement base, but the finish does not provide enough traction for the dancer. The chances of tendonitis from the dance surface are increased if the dancer is also not working correctly, but even flawless technique on this type of floor can't always prevent something from getting tight.

It is more likely, though, that incorrect technique will set up the conditions for tendonitis when the dancer is young. If you are going to the outside of the foot, concentrating the pressure on the edge of the heel to the small toe and not using the rest of the toes on the floor through the metatarsal to get to the middle of the foot, this can cause tendonitis in the arch and foot. If you are working toward the inside of the foot so that your ankle is leaning in over your heel, and you are putting pressure only on the big toe, and not utilizing the rest of the toes through the metatarsal, this can create tendonitis in the inside ankle, the foot itself, or in the upper arch. If you work through the middle of your foot, using the metatarsal and all the toes, but concentrate the weight on the heel, this can cause tendonitis in the back of the heel.

Perfect balance of the foot means using the foot completely. The proper way to stand is to have the whole foot on the floor, pressure on all the toes, and the arch lifted. When you are going through the movement of a *relevé*, you should be lifting the heel off the floor and going up through the metatarsal, pressing all the toes on the floor, and lifting up onto the toes, regardless of whether your toes are straight across or diagonal. It is crucial for the dancer to learn how to use the underneath part of the toes beyond the ball of the foot, and not everyone is able to teach dancers this. A dancer must be aware of how she is being taught—that she has to move carefully, as if placing her foot on an egg without cracking it.

Tendonitis can also come from jumping incorrectly. The dancer must land like a cat, and he or she must elongate the foot, landing on the toes, going through the metatarsal, and holding the weight on the thighs with straight knees. Gripping the toes tightens the back of the heel and can cause tremendous problems in the Achilles tendon area.

Incorrectly fitting pointe shoes can also create tendonitis in the foot and ankle. If you can't *relevé* up in new pointe shoes through the metatarsal with toes straight into the box of the shoe and the knees pulled up straight, your shoes probably don't fit you properly. Shoes that squeeze the toes, are too tight, or that cut into the upper metatarsal can cause tendonitis of the arch. If the heel of the shoe is loose, you will have to overgrip some part of the foot to *relevé*. If it is too tight, you can't get on your pointes through half pointe position. You shouldn't be going from the floor to your toes in a jumping movement, but through half pointe to pointe, using the full flexibility of the foot, just as you do when walking or running. The stress of going to pointe like a mechanical doll can cause tendonitis.

Finally, in terms of your training and tendonitis, if you are being taught to turn the inside or the outside of your ankles too much, you can overstretch the tendons. Often a teacher exaggerates the stretch of the inside of the ankle, and in people with loose ankles this can create more weakness than strength. Too great a turnout of your feet may mean that the upper part of your leg and the upper part of your body are out of balance. Check your turnout position from the foot to the knee, thigh, and hip. Your body should be in balance over the feet, the spine in one straight line. Don't turn out your feet to such an angle that your knee isn't over your toe. The turnout of the foot should be in relation to the turnout of the rest of the leg. You cannot use one part of your leg to turn out, and students who exaggerate one part of the turnout of the leg are very likely going to end up with tendonitis in some part of the foot or leg—the kind of tendonitis that should *never* happen if teacher and student are doing their proper jobs of giving and taking.

One last word on causes of tendonitis: It may not have anything to do with either training or shoes, with the floor or with fatigue. It may be due to an organic problem, such as a bone spur in the ankle or foot that is rubbing against a tendon. The only way a bone spur can be discovered is through X rays, and X rays taken at several different angles at that, since the spur may be very tiny. A spur may require an operation, but after you have checked into all possible causes of tendonitis, made an effort to correct them, and still suffer from it, you have to consider the possibility of a bone spur and take your case to a doctor.

Tracking down the cause of tendonitis is part of the cure, but the immediate problem is what to do when that sharp, paralyzing pain occurs. First of all, don't continue working in the same way, at the same pace, even though the pain diminishes and disappears as you work. The cause is still there, and you will simply be maintaining or aggravating the conditions that inflamed the tendon in the first place.

Usually, you should see a doctor, preferably an orthopedic doctor who is familiar with dancers' or at least athletes' injuries. (I'll talk about dancers' doctors at greater length in the next chapter.) He or she will probably tell you to rest, and he may prescribe an anti-inflammatory medication for a *short* time. Don't assume that you can safely continue to take the medication for a longer period than the ten days or less it is prescribed for. If the doctor keeps you on the medication for longer than ten days without giving you excellent reasons, he or she is probably not fully aware of the conditions of a dancer's life, and is treating you in terms of the general population, who do not have to rely on having their bodies in perfect working order for strenuous physical activity. The anti-inflammatory medication can become a crutch for the dancer; it may reduce the inflammation, but it doesn't

Sitting into heel.

Lifted-off heel.

Going through metatarsal.

Stretched in the air.

alter the cause. The same is true if the tendonitis is caused by a bone spur. If an operation is not advisable, some dancers turn to chiropractors to make sure the foot is properly aligned and the muscles are built up so that the irritation of the tendon doesn't recur. Chiropractors can help in the readjustment of feet and ankles so that the healing process is quicker, but no chiropractor, doctor, or podiatrist can correct the cause of tendonitis, which is your responsibility as a dancer to discover.

Special attention must be paid to the Achilles tendon, which is attached to the calf muscles that run down the back of the leg to the heel bone. If you have pain in the Achilles area, if it is swollen or sore, stop dancing at once, and see a doctor. A torn or stretched Achilles tendon is serious, and a ruptured Achilles tendon, where the fibers that attach tendon to bone are torn, may have to be repaired by surgery. The operation may not affect your walking ability, but it can affect your ability to dance, and often does. Many dancers' (and athletes') careers have been finished in an instant by the fact that the Achilles tendon snapped. It may not even hurt, but in the operation to correct it, the dancer almost invariably loses the elasticity that is so important in jumping and in the strength of the ankle.

For a stressed Achilles tendon, before the situation becomes too severe, the usual treatment is rest. And this means *rest*, for as long as the doctor tells you. Don't go back to work or training until it is completely healed, and when you start working again, do it slowly—and investigate closely the conditions of training, dance surface, or accident that led up to the Achilles problem.

Broken Bones

Years ago, when I was rehearsing with an inexperienced partner, he was holding me in a lift when he dropped me from the height of his arms. I broke my foot cleanly across the arch. Another time, I was practicing a series of *entrechats* when I was very tired, and I landed on the outside of my foot and broke my little toe. (Lest the reader think from my recital of illustrative injuries that I am especially accident prone, compared to many dancers I have had very few problems, and have never injured myself while onstage.)

The point is, the dancer is most vulnerable to injury when he or she is tired, and many dancers have suffered a broken bone somewhere in the foot sometime. (When Nureyev broke his toe late in 1979—onstage—it was considered a newsworthy event by the media!)

In the case of my broken foot, since it was a clean break across the arch with no involvement of tendons or ligaments, I was able to be back working in ten days. It was painful, but because the orthopedic doctor who treated me was aware of dancers' injuries, he gave me a bandage cast rather than a plaster one, which would have immobilized not only the bone but the muscles for too long. A regular cast might be exactly right for a nondancer who has a similar break and, of course, might be necessary even for a dancer with a complicated injury, but you have to be able to discuss your special situation with your doctor and know that he understands it. In the case of my broken foot, my doctor was experienced enough with dancers to know what was needed.

In the case of my broken toe, the advice I got resulted in a less happy conclusion—some twenty years later. The break was originally diagnosed as a sprain, not a broken bone, although the wisdom gained from years of dancing would tell me now that I couldn't have been back dancing in a couple of weeks as I was with a sprain, although it's certainly possible with a broken toe. The break healed on its own, but not properly, and over the years a cyst formed at the break without pain. The traumatized area eventually developed blood poisoning (naturally, on the eve of an important performance in Dallas, far away from my regular doctor). Emergency treatment enabled me to perform, but I required a serious operation after the cyst was diagnosed as a tumor. My performing career might have ended then, but fortunately it did not, as no nerves were damaged, either by the injury or the operation.

A good diagnosis is as important as the treatment. Sprains (which I'll talk about in more detail in the next chapter) are painful enough to keep you from dancing until the injury has healed. You can go back to dancing, as I did, on a broken toe, with some pain, quite soon after the event.

The Male Dancer's Feet

Foot care, toughening and conditioning the skin, and nail care are very important to both men and women dancers, and men working incorrectly are as susceptible as women to tendonitis in various areas of the foot and ankle. The conditioning that relates directly to working on pointe is not a major concern for men, but working on pointe can help a man's feet. It stretches the tendons of the arch, gives a better shape to the foot, and strengthens the ankles, which I believe some male dancers need. They have such marvelous strength in their thighs and calves, but they often substitute that strength for the trouble of going through the whole leg because feet and ankles are not equally strong. If they are required to focus on their feet, as in working on pointe, they can develop strength—and it can be fun.

Men do have to remember that for them, the possibility of sprained or broken toes or feet is more common because they do more frequent and energetic jumps than women. Bad jumps that can result in injuries may be caused by a weakness in ankles or feet. When a dancer lands from any jump, toe to heel, the ankle and thigh take tremendous pressure and must be strong.

Male dancers may also have tight arches or flat feet. Neither situation is impossible to correct, and the exercises for feet given below are often helpful.

Exercises for the Feet

Both men and women dancers need to have strong feet, ankles, and toes. When I was a young dancer, my teacher once asked me to put my foot into his hand and press as hard as I could with my toes. I already knew I had strong feet; what the demonstration proved to me was that I didn't have strong toes—and that was where I danced, from the tips of my toes to the top of my head. If I had a problem stretching my toes when I was doing a *tendu*, if I wasn't really able to support myself when I landed from a jump, then my toes weren't strong enough.

It isn't enough to shrug and say, "Well, that's the way I am. So my toes aren't strong or I have tight arches." Every dancer has to learn to ask questions, and to listen to the answers he or she gets.

The first question to ask is, "What can I do to change or improve?"

In the case of how to have stronger toes, I started asking other dancers. Rosella Hightower suggested, "Put a towel on the floor and knead it the way a cat kneads with its feet."

I tried it. It helped strengthen my toes (it's also good for tight arches and flat feet). Try kneading with a towel, and if you get a cramp, don't do it as quickly, but do it often during the day. Also try picking up the towel with your toes, holding for a count of five, and releasing. I went on to picking up a pencil with my toes and dropping it, and finally to marbles, which is one of the most effective ways to strengthen the toes. Learn to pick up a marble with each toe, moving each toe separately, the way you can move individual fingers. If you're starting with weak toes and a weak metatarsal, you have to work up to this point gradually. Get to the point where each toe can hold a marble for the count of five before releasing. (This is a good exercise for men with flat feet or tight arches.)

Tired arches from working hard can be relieved and the arch strengthened by rolling the foot over a small bottle or juice can. Some dance shops also sell rollers designed for exercising arches and toes which serve the same purpose.

When you realize that there is a weakness in your toes and feet, you can work on the problem in warming up before class at the barre. Do *pliés* and *relevés* on one foot and then the other: a small *plié*, pressing from the toe, working from the toe to the heel, and making sure that the knee is over the toe. *Relevé*, lifting the heels from the floor, through the metatarsal to the toes, which are pressed firmly to the floor—the same distance up as down (don't do a deep *plié*). Do this about fifteen or twenty times on each foot, alternating feet. If you don't feel secure doing it on one foot at first, do it on both feet as you begin. Don't allow the calves to tighten. Even though this is the type of movement you will be doing in class, a concentrated movement without tiring yourself is very strengthening for feet and ankles. Strong feet and ankles are also important for modern dancers, who can use this exercise to good advantage.

8

ACHES AND INJURIES

The esthetic creation of what dance is supposed to be won't happen overnight; the dancer has steps to go through before this occurs. But he or she has to be excited about what there is to be discovered.

This includes matters so mundane and so important as the overall condition of the body. You have to take as much pride in prevention of injuries as you do in achieving a difficult combination. Asking questions and finding answers about everything to do with dance is part of the essential preparation to be a dancer. If you are willing to devote yourself fully to the discipline of dance, you must keep asking yourself what your training means. If you are aware of a hurt or a weakness or if you have constant injuries, you have to ask yourself whether you are exaggerating or misunderstanding what your teacher is telling you. You should never hesitate to ask the teacher why something is happening or to help you correct what you think might be the problem. But for young dancers, it's difficult even to know if there is a problem.

Students come to me and say, "Can you help me with my turnout?" or "Could you help me with my arabesque line?" It's not a problem with an arabesque line; something else is causing the arabesque line not to happen. I—the teacher—can define how, where, and what the problem is, but it is essential for the dancer to learn awareness of a weakness, what its implications might be, and then *ask questions*.

The responsibility is to your body and your art. This means undergoing the process of realization that dance is a *physical* matter, not something that happens in the mind. The muscles you use are in a state of conditioning; often they get tired, and there is an ache. Growing pains happen in the formation of the muscles. At some time in the past, a muscle was not functioning for you; now, all of a sudden, it is. It's saying, with the ache, "Here I am."

It doesn't matter how much you understand in your head about dancing. It's what your muscles understand. They know the difference between pain and the ache of learning. Pain exists for the dancer only to tell him or her that something is wrong, that the body has been damaged or is defending itself against damage.

I don't think a young dancer should spend several years in training and still have to ask, "Why am I aching?" Yet I find myself too often telling students that, yes, conditioning of the body causes the muscles to respond in ways that are not always comfortable, but should never be painful.

"My thighs are killing me. Is that good?"

Yes, it's good. The muscles of the thigh haven't been fully trained before; they're learning new muscle memory now that you're using your whole leg to dance.

"The insides of my legs hurt. Why do they feel so tight?"

Again, when the muscles have formed, the soreness will go away.

"I have a muscle on the side of my foot that aches, and it seems to be bigger than it used to be. Is that good?"

The muscles of the foot are being formed and strengthened. You're using your foot properly.

If you can walk and sit without pain, then the ache of muscles after working is a good kind of ache that tells you there is growth, that a muscle is learning a new memory to help you dance, the kind of memory that your body performs automatically when your teacher or the choreographer calls out the combinations you must dance.

After three months, she finally began to ask "how to."

Only if your muscles don't function after you've warmed up, if the soreness continues for more than a couple of days and bathing and massage don't help, and if the sensation is more than soreness but real pain, is your body telling you that all is not well. You've injured yourself or have developed a condition such as tendonitis. The pain is telling you to stop and find out what's wrong before further damage is done.

Dance—whether classical ballet, modern dance, jazz, or any permutation or combination—should not be painful. The dancer who works in pain is not being heroic; he or she is foolish, and, more than foolish, has failed in the responsibility each dancer has to be aware of the instrument, and to take proper care of it.

Sprains and Tendonitis

In the previous chapter, I spoke of tendonitis and sprains as they occur in the dancer's feet. Both occur in other parts of the leg as well, although perhaps less frequently. Tendonitis, you must remember, is characterized by pain that diminishes as you begin to work, and the dancer may want to believe that the source of the pain has "gone away." It hasn't. It will happen again, the next time you start to dance, and again, until the body refuses to undergo more trauma and the area is paralyzed. The cure is rest, and correction of the faulty technique that is usually the cause of tendonitis.

With a sprain, the dancer can't even hope that the pain will lessen with working. You have to stop dancing, treat the sprain, and rest. It may be not just that the fibers connecting muscle, tendon, and bone have been torn, but that the tendon may be becoming stretched. If you go back to dancing before the healing process is complete, you may overstretch the tendons, and overstretched tendons do not go back to normal. A dancer with an overstretched tendon around the ankle may be able to go back to performing for a while, but eventually the work, and especially fatigue in the muscles in the area formed to support the tendon, will cause those muscles to wear down. The dancer loses any hope of being that complete instrument for dance, and must face the fact that with the capacity for working diminished, the capacity for expression decreases.

When you sprain an ankle or toe (or any other part of the body), the area will usually swell with discoloration. The best immediate first aid is to put an ice pack on the area and elevate it. Sometimes such injuries can be temporarily helped if you put a compress of undiluted Burow's Solution on the area and wrap it in ordinary plastic food wrap for an hour. Alternate this with ice until the swelling goes down. When the swelling has been alleviated, continue with the Burow's Solution and bathing in tepid water, but see that you have the sprain examined by a doctor within twenty-four hours (you cannot risk the possibility that a broken bone is involved in the injury). *Don't ignore any injury.*

This first aid treatment is one of the dancer's home remedies, which doctors have called an effective emergency measure. The sprained area will ache, but the compress of Burow's Solution draws out the inflammation and allows blood to circulate and heal the injury. The bruise that develops will probably spread, and instead of being just black and blue, will become a multicolored orange and yellow. Don't be alarmed—it's an indication that the sprain is in the process of healing.

Shin Splints

Shin splints are an inflammation of the muscles and tendons in the lower leg, usually the front, but sometimes the inside and outside of the leg. They are another common dancer's ailment that shouldn't happen.

The pain of shin splints can be intense, and is usually a generalized area of pain rather than a specific one near the middle of the shin or close to the ankle. The dancer does not usually lose coordination. However, I must digress here to the matter of hair fractures, which initially are sometimes mistaken for shin splints. The pain from a hair fracture is usually in a specific area, but you can work for a time with a fracture. It does not impede movement, even though the pain may be sharp until the dancer is warmed up. But if the fracture isn't treated, the dancer can lose muscle function and coordination, even if the fracture heals. If you feel a loss of coordination with what you think to be shin splints and have treated as such, have the area X-rayed at once for a possible hair fracture. The treatment is rest, as much as three weeks, but follow doctor's orders and do not dance until the fracture has healed.

If you believe that the pain you feel is shin splints, you have to determine what is causing them. Although shin splints may sometimes be traced to the floor surface the dancer works on (a hard wood over cement surface, for example), the usual cause is incorrect dance technique that puts pressure on the tendons and muscles in the shin.

Landing incorrectly from jumps can cause shin splints. Check your training. Do you come through the heel very quickly when you land? Do you land on your heel instead of going through the toes and metatarsal and using your thighs? The bulk of the pressure should be taken on the thighs above the knee.

Standing incorrectly is probably the most common cause of shin splints. Students who develop the problem often stand and dance on the outside of the foot only, gripping with the outside of the toes, pressing on the outside of the heel, and do not work to the middle of the whole foot as they should. This puts pressure on the outside of the shin.

Your teacher may observe this and help to correct it (but if you are wearing practice clothes that camouflage the way you stand, he or she won't be able to see the problem). You can check yourself on the way you're standing. Look at the bottom of your ballet slippers or toe shoes. A shoe that's been worn for a while will pick up dirt from the floor. If you are standing properly on the whole foot, the wear will be evenly distributed around the edge of the shoe. If you see that the bottom of the shoe is darkened just on the outside from the heel to the little toe, you are working and standing incorrectly to the side rather than in the middle of the foot. When this happens, not only is pressure put on the shin area, but the upper body is not placed over the hips, so that the dancer often leans too far forward for balance. A tension is created in the upper body, or the shoulders are tensed.

Dancers on pointe who show a similar pattern of wear are possibly rolling to the outside of the foot so that the tendon over the outside of the ankle is being stretched. Usually, in this case, the body is placed back to find a balance, again rather than straight over the hips.

The treatment for shin splints, besides determining the cause and taking steps to correct it, is heat, preferably warm baths rather than hot showers; hot, damp cloths on the area; warmth from extra socks when you're outdoors, especially in winter. (Warm coverings during class may be worn too—as long as they don't hide what you're trying to correct.) Commercial medications that you can rub on the area to numb the pain are tempting to use. They may give temporary relief, but deadening the pain doesn't cure the ailment. The anesthetic properties ease discomfort, but they don't heal the inflamed muscles and tendons, and in the long run such medications are dangerous because it's too easy to forget about the problem when the pain goes away.

If the shin splints don't heal within ten days or a couple of weeks with treatment and correction of their cause, see a doctor in case there is a hair fracture or a circulation problem. Remember that reducing diets, with a diminished vitamin and mineral supply, can cause leg pains that might be mistaken for shin splints.

When my students say, "My shins are beginning to bother me, I must be standing on the wrong part of my foot," they're developing the kind of awareness of their bodies no dancer should be without. They're accepting the responsibility for educating themselves and learning to take an active part in correcting and healing themselves instead of relying wholly on doctors.

Knees and the Dancer

Dancers (and all athletes) fear knee injuries more than almost any other kind. Such injuries are difficult to treat successfully, since the knees are not joints the way hips, for example, are. Rather, the knee is the point where two long bones that form the upper and lower leg are held together with tendons and ligaments instead of being set in a socket. Of necessity, and largely because of developments in sports medicine, corrective knee surgery has become quite common. But the result is very often a patient who can walk, but can no longer dance—

or play football, tennis, hockey, or basketball. There have been, to be sure, many successful knee operations on many, many dancers and athletes, but I believe that no operation is the best operation. Besides the possible physical incapacity, there is a deep psychological effect. The dancer who has undergone a knee operation is always going to be aware of the fact, and will hold back involuntarily from executing properly the movement he or she wishes to accomplish. The dancer has grown up in dance striving to experience something through movement, and finally when he or she is technically able to do it, these kinds of operations bring home the realization that they can't do it quite the same way.

Thus, any indication of a knee problem must be investigated immediately. Very young dancers shouldn't have any knee problems. When a knee bothers a young dancer, it may be simply a matter of physical growth—in the early and mid-teens, growing pains are not unexpected. But if the knee problem is dance-related, it is probably because the training stresses the turnout from the inside of the knee too much and does not encourage the turnout through the upper thigh and the whole leg. If the dancer overextends the turnout of the feet but the hips are not turned out enough, the muscles of the thigh in a young dancer are not strong enough to hold the turnout, and pressure is put on the knees.

Dancers who are a little older can't be too careful about knee pain, and certainly if a dancer has had considerable training and then develops pain in the knee, he or she should immediately discover the reason and see that the condition is corrected. My experience with dancers and knee problems has been that often they do not *plié* properly. They go right into the knee in the *plié* instead of holding the weight of the body on the thigh to the toes.

When you extend your leg to the back, especially in a *tendu* or *temps lié*, you can overstretch the tendon in the knee if you turn out too much from the inside of the knee and the thigh is not over the toe. When the dancer is young, this is simply an annoyance. It might hurt some, but the dancer can continue to work and the pain may go away because the movement becomes a muscle memory and the body adjusts to it. When the dancer is older, however, in the late teens and after, the pattern established for those tendons and muscles becomes a

Never overextend yourself.

weakness. Everything is going beautifully, but the weakness innocently created years before now becomes a detriment to dancing and finally an injury from which there may be less than perfect recovery.

Any indication of knee problems, even though they don't curtail movement, must be investigated. It's real preventive medicine to examine the training, and in the case of older dancers, to make a strenuous effort not to allow conditions causing knee problems to continue.

If your knee swells and you have pain in any part of the knee, you have probably stretched the cartilage itself. See an orthopedic doctor at once, and follow orders for resting the knee and applying ice packs. However, if the doctor suggests that you work through a knee injury, I believe you should strongly question the advice. Almost no doctor who is experienced in treating dancers or athletes will suggest you do this.

After you have rested the knee for ten days or so, as will probably be advised, and have returned to work only to find that the pain and swelling recur, the diagnosis may have been incorrect. There may be a tear in the cartilage which will require further treatment; it will not heal if it is continually stressed by further dancing. At one point in my career I did have an overstretched cartilage in my knee, and I listened to the advice of the excellent doctor who told me to rest. However, the cartilage never did go back to its original size, and I was aware that I could never really stretch my turnout as in the past. I worked slowly to develop my thigh muscles to compensate and to make certain that the pressure in dancing was not on the knee. Part of the effort was inspired by the warning that if the condition recurred once more, after it had happened twice, I would probably tear the cartilage and have to undergo an operation.

Although injections of cortisone and the like are sometimes prescribed for joint and knee injuries, I am extremely wary of this type of anti-inflammatory medication. It may help for the moment, but I have too often seen the kind of permanent weakness that can develop from repeated injections. Years later, the joint has become such a weak point that a misstep off a curb can result in a broken bone rather than a sprain.

No doctor who is truly experienced in treating dancers or athletes routinely prescribes cortisone injections, and you have the right and obligation to question a physician who suggests them for knee injuries or joint problems. You, after all, may be dealing in terms of an entire career, and certainly with your desire to dance, in which you have already invested a good deal of time and effort and physical and emotional energy. This is not to say that cortisone and similar medicines are not necessarily appropriate for the public at large; but dance medicine is different. The young dancer is somewhat at the mercy of older and theoretically more experienced individuals—a father who says injections helped him, a doctor who has successfully used anti-inflammatory medications in his practice. But neither one is a dancer or fully aware of the dancer's needs. Remember your right to ask questions and to get satisfactory answers about any treatment suggested for you.

Although knee injuries can occur in women dancers when they are getting up on pointe, when they are trying to get their hips over their toes but the knees are not straight and are really in a relaxed position, the male dancer is far more likely to have knee injuries because of the strain of jumping and partnering. In modern dance, knee injuries may be related to falls, which are part of the technique. If the dancer is well trained, such injuries can be avoided, but if the thighs are not aligned over the whole foot in jumps, the knee can be damaged. If the dancer doesn't *plié* properly when lifting a partner and coming down, strain is put on the knees as well as the back. Brute force in lifting a partner is not enough; ideally, the woman partner is strong enough to support herself and not put the entire burden on the man.

Men, too, have a tendency to be tighter in their hips than women, so their turnout is tighter. Be sure that the teacher doesn't force you to turn out the inside of the knee until you are ready, or the result may be a knee injury caused by the constant stress of the turnout or overstretched ligaments.

Hips and Back

A proper turnout for both men and women does not come from forcing; it comes from doing movement naturally and correctly. Some people are born loose-limbed and are able to stand in a very turned-out position in each of the five positions. Others are tight hipped, and their legs don't rotate easily. They have to work gradually toward a proper rotation, concentrating on the alignment of their thighs under their hips. To be a good dancer, you don't have to have a natural turn-out, although it helps; you can acquire a proper turnout through training and through the exercises themselves. Be wary of a training that forces the turnout if you are naturally tight hipped. You do not want to traumatize the tendons in the front part of the hips, forcing them forward, or at the top of the leg. This can cause chronic hip problems, and you may be unable to move one way or the other. Remember that the whole leg is involved in the turnout, including the back of the leg, which is important in holding the rotation of the thigh.

Hip problems can also develop in dancers who are encouraged to tuck under too much, forcing the pelvic bone forward and changing the natural line of the spine. This is especially a problem if the individual has a natural curve to the spine. There is no way in ballet or other dance training that you can change the back you were born with by tucking under (although a curvature of the spine may be corrected by therapy). Forcing a change in the back can result in a weakness in the lower lumbar region, and in jumping, the dancer can wear out the discs in the lower spine if too much pressure is put on them instead of on the thigh and the whole leg (worn discs are a problem with many dancers).

Back injuries in men are often the result of being taught to lift partners improperly. Here it is important for the male dancer to be taught by someone who is experienced in the techniques of partnering. Therapeutic exercises can be very helpful for developing back and arm strength. Pushups and other exercises that consist of holding the diaphragm and stomach muscles are good. I often suggest that young men lie flat on their backs with their feet two inches off the floor. They raise their feet to a forty-five-degree angle from the floor, hold to the count of five, then lower them again to two inches from the floor for another count of five. Do this twice a day, ten times. There is a direct reaction in the abdominal muscles, and in a very short time the dancer will get stronger. Don't use ankle weights for this exercise, as this is too much of a good thing. This exercise is also excellent for developing strength in the stomach muscles and lower back of women dancers, but I feel an exercise of this type is imperative for men, who too often ignore the lower back.

Sometimes a dancer has a problem with ankles or knees and can't figure out the cause. If all else fails, it's a good idea to see an orthopedic doctor or chiropractor who can check out the alignment of the back with X rays. Improper back alignment may first manifest itself in ankles or knees because the dancer is favoring one leg over the other. In fact, for dancers with knee problems, the healing may start with back corrections with the aid of a chiropractor.

Shoulders, Neck, Arms

If you find that your shoulders are not aligned, it may be that one leg is longer than the other. This is not uncommon; few people are born with both sides of the body completely equal, and there are few dancers who feel comfortable on both sides naturally. If one leg is a somewhat different length from the other, you have to make the effort to equalize the strength in both sides so that both work together strongly—but not necessarily identically. You cannot make one side work exactly like the other, but each can work individually yet harmoniously.

Sometimes a dancer has naturally tight shoulders. In dancing, the arms and shoulders should be comfortably held, and if you find that you can't keep your shoulders down, it may be due to tight pectoral muscles. It is better in such a case to use therapy to loosen the muscles rather than to stress other parts of the body in an effort to keep the shoulders down, which will only displace the body's alignment. Therapists can suggest arm exercises to stretch the pectoral muscles, sometimes with weights on the shoulders. In any kind of therapeutic exercise, however, everything should be done in moderation, either under supervision or following the instructions of the therapist.

Neck problems can occur in dancers when they are not working properly in a pirouette, particularly when they overturn the head. A snapping of the head in a turn can traumatize the vertebrae in the neck and put them out of alignment. I experienced this once because I was doing a variation to music that was too fast. In keeping up with the music, my head had to spot faster than I ordinarily would in pirouettes, and I whipped my neck out of place, which required a visit to the doctor and rest to put right.

The student who is afraid to spot or to look in a pirouette is probably reacting involuntarily to past or present pain in the neck when performing the movement. A pirouette should be as easy as walking. If you are frightened of doing pirouettes, ask yourself why. Go back to the way you were trained to do pirouettes, and you may find that at some point the movement was painful, and so now, whether you have a pain or not, you do not release your neck so that your head can turn along with the body. If the neck vertebrae are actually out of alignment they can be readjusted, and an understanding teacher can help you learn to do pirouettes properly, without fear or hesitation.

In *port de bras* to the back, the head shouldn't be dropped from the neck. It's a *stretch* to the back, the back holds the hips in place, and the vertebrae arch to the back from the top of the chest so the neck does not drop. Be aware that if you *port de bras* forward with the body over the front of the toes, the head is the first to go down and the last to come up, which takes the pressure off the lower back.

Doctors and Dancers

A dancer should learn to question anything that's done by a doctor about his or her injuries, not to be difficult or belligerent or to do the doctor's job, but to have a full understanding of what is taking place in terms of the injury and the treatment. In five or ten years, it may turn out to be very important that you know what was done and why. You should have a rapport with the doctor so that there is open communication. Some doctors (and I have encountered them myself) dislike being questioned, and this can set up a negative relationship, with the intimidated dancer failing to get the information he or she should have.

You should feel free to ask such questions as: Why did this injury happen to me? What are you doing to treat it? How long will it take to heal? Will it occur again? How can I avoid this type of injury?

What are the effects and side effects of prescribed medication? Will this injury have any long-range effect on my dancing?

If the doctor you are consulting isn't interested in educating you about your body, he or she is probably not the ideal doctor for the dancer.

Dancers usually require an orthopedic specialist, and should attempt to find one who is accustomed to treating dancers. It's a good idea, too, to find a doctor before you need one, rather than picking one when there's an emergency. In a city like New York or San Francisco or Dallas, or elsewhere where there are a lot of dancers, it shouldn't be too difficult to find a doctor who deals with dance injuries. You can ask your teacher or other students for recommendations, or find out who treats the dancers in the resident ballet company if there is one.

Failing to find a doctor who is experienced in treating dancers, you should seek out one who treats athletes, since they have similar types of injuries. In most smaller cities and towns, there is likely to be a doctor who regularly treats the athletes on college or high school sports teams. Sports medicine is a growing specialty. More and more doctors are becoming aware of the kinds of injuries suffered by people engaged in strenuous physical activity and the treatment they need, which may differ from that required by the general public.

Sports medicine is also developing new techniques and equipment (thanks very much to professional sports, where there is a huge investment in the health of athletes) to bring injured players back to form. It is entirely possible that such techniques and equipment can be applied now to dancers' injuries by a knowledgeable sports or dance doctor, but they certainly will be in the future. If you can't find an orthopedist who treats dancers, and wish to locate a sports medicine specialist in your area, the American Orthopaedic Society for Sports Medicine (430 North Michigan Avenue, Chicago, Illinois 60611) has a list of society members throughout the United States.

Chiropractors are a touchy subject with some people, but many dancers, myself included, have come to rely on them for adjusting the structural balance of the body when necessary to make it possible to dance. On the other hand, don't feel falsely secure in the treatment from a chiropractor. If you feel better but have to be treated continuously and there is no chronic injury, you are using the chiropractor as a crutch, and the injury is not being treated properly. Chiropractic treatment shouldn't last forever.

Whether or not to use the services of a chiropractor is an individual decision. Children and teenagers shouldn't see a chiropractor without their parents' permission, and don't assume that just because you are a dancer, you must be treated by one. A lot of dancers never see a chiropractor throughout their entire dancing lives.

Again, any chiropractor a dancer sees should be experienced in treating dancers. Talk to people who know—your teacher, more experienced dancers. For the young dancer, unless he or she has overextended in a jump, there's a sharp pain on landing, or a worn disc, occasions to see a chiropractor should be rare.

Health insurance is part of the necessary expense of being a dancer, like shoes and leotards. Many family health insurance plans stop coverage of a young person at about the age of nineteen, and it's essential that individual coverage be picked up at that time. Be sure you know what the insurance covers. What kind of provision is made for X rays, for example, since dancers may require more X rays than nondancers? Are chiropractors included? (In some states, they are not.) If you are leaving your home state for a period of study in New York or elsewhere, will your insurance coverage be valid wherever you are?

Nowadays, people are increasingly concerned about X rays and the cumulative effect of X-ray radiation. With the development of high-speed X-ray film in recent years, the period of exposure has been reduced. I do not suggest that anyone undergo X rays for the slightest reason, but they are an essential diagnostic tool for dancer's injuries, and are the only way a physician can discover hair fractures, bone spurs, and other conditions that could hamper dancing or even put a stop to it if left untreated.

Medications for Dancers

I've mentioned several kinds of medications commonly used by dancers, along with some commonsense home remedies and over-the-counter products. Here's a brief checklist of what they are and what they can do for you:

Tincture of Merthiolate: Used on tender toe skin to help toughen and condition the area, and to act as an antiseptic to prevent infection.

Medicated foot powder: Used regularly after bathing to prevent infection and to help condition the feet.

Burow's Solution: Used on compresses for sprains (with the area wrapped in plastic food wrap).

Numbing creams and ointments: These are local anesthetics that deaden pain; they give temporary relief, but should be used sparingly, as they do not heal or cure the cause of the pain.

Cortisone (steroid) injections: These are prescribed for joint and knee injuries. Cortisone, however, may be a doubtful treatment for dancers' and athletes' injuries because the temporary relief is offset by the possibility of later weakness in the affected joint. Question use closely.

Anti-inflammatory medications: These are prescribed for tendonitis, and other injuries where muscles or tendons are inflamed. They are to be used by doctor's prescription and only for limited periods. Do not use leftovers from previous prescriptions to self-medicate. If there is an allergic or other reaction from the medication, stop taking it immediately.

Ice: Used to reduce swelling from knee injuries or ankle or other sprains. See an orthopedist, especially in the case of knee problems.

Heat: Used in the form of warm baths or hot, damp cloths for tendonitis and shin splints. Warm baths are also an ideal way to reduce soreness in muscles fatigued from working.

Rest: Used to good purpose in most kinds of injuries. Follow doctor's orders to rest injuries, even if you think you can work through them; don't try to get back to work sooner than prescribed. When you are told to rest, *rest*.

PART IV

The Dance Experience

9

BECOMING
A PROFESSIONAL

If you are a trained dancer, somewhere in this country there is an opportunity for you to dance.

Some people call getting that chance to dance "luck."

It looks like luck to an outsider, being in the right place at the right time, finding out at the last minute that there's an audition, showing up and dancing your best that day so that you stand out from the hundreds of others who want the same job.

It may be luck, but if it is, it has been made by the dancer.

People have said to me, "Isn't it lucky that when you needed a job in order to stay on in New York, you found one." Or, "Isn't it lucky that Balanchine asked you to join the New York City Ballet"; or, "Isn't it lucky that you were chosen to dance in this ballet or that."

I think, in the end, that I don't believe in luck. I believe in *intention*. I believe in the necessity of having the dream. And I believe very much in the power of having a positive attitude. With these—and

The desire to dance is not enough; you have to shape and focus it.

Getting there.

Arriving.

preparation—you make your own luck. Preparation encompasses everything I've been talking about: learning technique, learning how to make sentences in dance, being a whole person, knowing how your body works, how to take care of it, what to do when you're injured, having your shoes broken in when you need them, and being able to find in your practice bag anything you need in an emergency.

Your intention must be strong, your preparation perfect, and then you will know how to be in the right place at the right time, able to show your abilities in the right way to people who want you to dance for them, and for an audience.

Between having the desire to dance and learning how, and actually being a dancer who is paid to perform before an audience, is the process of being hired. Almost every young dancer in training has at least a hope at some point of bringing the dream to its logical end by performing. The image that he or she has been creating all these years always means a belief in one's ability to dance effectively for an audience, and more than just occasionally.

As the dancer's training brings him or her closer to having that complete instrument, the need to examine goals becomes more urgent. You have to start making your own luck—by preparing yourself to be judged not by a teacher, but by professional standards. For the student dancer studying in a major center like New York, just being a part of this world gives some insight into the workings of the business, through meeting and working with other dancers who may have had a wider range of experiences they can share. And it pays to listen. My words and my advice are only one person's opinion—based, to be sure, on long and varied experience in the dance world. As such, it is accurate. But everyone has a slightly different image and goal; everyone's circumstances, strengths, weaknesses, and tastes are qualities that determine where he or she will be happy and how far the desire to dance will lead.

The young dancer has to make some hard decisions about his or her self-image—and answer some essential questions about the future that looms nearer as technique and artistry become more polished:

"Do I really want to make my living as a dancer, or should dance be an avocation rather than a career? Or should I investigate other areas where I can use my dance training?"

"Am I happy in a highly competitive place like New York, or would

I feel more secure at home in familiar surroundings? And why New York? Do I like the cold climate? Would I be happier in another city, such as Houston or Tulsa or Atlanta, or on the West Coast?"

"Do I want to go home as a big fish and take over the pond, or do I want to try to start with a small dance company, wherever a job is available, and work toward something bigger? Can I take the risk of failing or succeeding? Am I going to be able to accept the growing pains and the ego trips I'm going to have to go through?"

And finally, "Am I really good enough to be paid to dance? Am I willing to put myself, and all those years of training, on the line? Will people look at me and say, 'You're worth what they're paying you.' ?"

The last question is really the beginning for anyone who wants to get a job as a dancer. The only way you can find out is to try.

The decision to audition as a professional means that you have added a new dimension to your image as a dancer. You are cutting yourself away from the comfort and security of your student role and stepping out into the world. And not because you need the money, not because you've said to yourself, "I've studied for this many years, so it's time to get a job." Rather, you have to come to the point where you say to yourself, "It's time to get a job, because I know I'm *ready.*"

Desire and preparation: these make a dancer.

The decision is reached at different points in different dancers' lives. Some are ready to make the step after a few months of advanced, concentrated study; others need a longer period of training or a longer time to focus their intentions. You have to be emotionally as well as technically prepared to audition. The people who head dance companies have different tastes and requirements, as I will discuss later at greater length. If you don't make it at an audition, you have to be able to understand that rejection here does not equal failure as a dancer.

Where the Jobs Are

The initial step for a young dancer who wants to perform is to know where to look for people who are looking for dancers. Show business is not an easy business; there are always more talented performers than there are openings, certainly in a city like New York. Dance is no different from any other branch of the theater. Fortunately, though, so much is going on in dance, all kinds of dance—ballet, modern, jazz, ethnic—all around the country today that a good dancer with sound training can, with intention, find a place to dance.

The starting point, of course, is still a major dance center where artistic directors of small companies seek the new dancers they need to add to their companies. Many artistic directors from around the country and abroad come to New York periodically to visit the various schools to look at the dancers; often they are steered to dancers who may fit their needs by dance teachers. Many artistic directors hold open auditions for student dancers.

It's up to you, though, to inform yourself as fully as possible, both about the companies themselves and the types of dancers they use, their repertoires, their style, and about where auditions are being held. As in looking for any kind of job, you need to find out all you can about a prospective employer—the artistic director, the performing schedule, the artistic philosophy. It's even a good idea to keep a notebook on companies and their repertoires. Word-of-mouth is one of the most useful sources of information about dance companies. It pays to make the acquaintance of dancers you're studying with, since many of them may have had experience, good or bad, with the companies in question; some may even be working dancers who are taking extra class at your studio. Word-of-mouth also brings you news of openings in a company, auditions that are being held, and so forth. School bulletin boards post times of auditions; they are also listed in theatrical newspapers (*Backstage, Show Business,* and *Variety* in New York).

Rarely does a job find a dancer to fill it; you have to make yourself available to be seen and judged and possibly hired. This means not only going to auditions, but dancing in workshops and demonstrations where you stand a chance of being seen by someone who has a job to offer.

Student dancers in regions of the country other than New York will find that touring companies from various states, many supported by the National Endowment for the Arts, hold open auditions when they pass through an area, as do some of the major New York-based companies when on tour. They look for new dancers who might be compatible with those already in the company, or they may offer scholarships for their apprentice programs.

A young dancer has to be realistic about such an offer, however, since a scholarship may not cover all the expenses of traveling to the city where the company is based and all living expenses. The excitement of being offered an apprentice scholarship can be dampened by facts of life; you have to be sure of adequate outside support if you accept an offer to join a company's apprentice program. You don't want to end up having to work at jobs other than dancing to support yourself. This takes away energy from what you want to be doing, which is dancing.

At one time, people seriously studying the arts went to Europe for polishing and for their first professional breaks. Opera singers still find opportunities abroad that aren't available in the United States (although this is becoming less true nowadays). But for dancers, dancing abroad is highly competitive, and most American dancers who perform with European companies are not beginning professionals, but seasoned dancers who have chosen to find a new dance experience in a different setting. Male dancers, of course, are always in demand everywhere in the world, so a young man stands a better chance of finding a job abroad than women dancers in general do.

Although there are many ballet companies in Europe—in England, France, Germany, Denmark, The Netherlands—some (the Royal Ballet in England, the Royal Danish Ballet, for example) only hire nationals of the country except for rare individuals with unique talent. Thus, although some dancers have been picked by foreign companies from American schools, student dancers have a far better chance of working professionally in the United States than they have out of the country.

Auditioning the Company

Part of the auditioning process consists of being considered by the choreographer or artistic director in terms of how you as a person will fit into the company, as well as on your abilities as a dancer. A good artistic director understands that a positive chemistry between people who have to work together in a creative endeavor is absolutely necessary. Thus, sometimes a lesser dancer will be chosen by the director because the chemistry seems right for the company, and a more accomplished dancer is passed over because the chemistry isn't there. This is not a rejection of the dancer or his or her talent; it's necessity on the part of the man or woman who has to have the best interests of the entire company in mind.

Young dancers concentrate on the fact of being chosen; it's nice to be wanted. Yet I believe that no matter how hungry you are—to have a job or to dance—and how eager to be a part of a ballet or modern dance company, you must, in a sense, audition that company and its artistic director. Learn to be objective about both your need to get a job and the people and environment you are going to be working with if you are hired. You have to know you're going to be reasonably content with the company, and you have to test and be satisfied with the chemistry as much as the director.

If you can get to know people who dance with the company or can find out something about it from dancers who have, you can get an idea of the conditions you'll be facing, the director's attitude toward dancers. Gather any bits of information you can to give you a picture of what the company is like. If you tie yourself to a contract to dance with a company you start out not liking or where you're uncomfortable, the next step is hating everything you're doing. This is not a way to dance, and dance well. If you don't like the other dancers, the environment, or the director, you'll resist the new choreography and the pressures of rehearsing and performing. You will become careless, and that is when you injure yourself. Which gives you a real excuse for not doing what you don't want to do.

The dance world, overall, is really quite small. If you have signed a piece of paper committing yourself to dance with a company where you're not happy, and when something better comes along you go to it without a second thought, the word-of-mouth is eventually going to be about you. A reputation for being a conscientious dancer who acts professionally is a valuable asset. It is not so good to be known as someone who fails to honor contracts, is temperamental, or resists the requirements of working within and with a company.

Remember that no experience as a dancer is wasted, even time with a company that isn't entirely what you believed it would be, where conditions are difficult perhaps, and the pay isn't high. Even a bad experience teaches you something, if only that it is not what you want as a dancer. Dancers are as vulnerable as anybody else to discouragement and unhappiness, but don't let any experience cripple you and tarnish your dreams.

About Dance Companies

The person who sets the policy, decides on the design of a company, chooses the dancers and the repertoire, and often does much of the choreography is the artistic director. He or she decides on the direction the development of the dancers should take. The attitude of the artistic director is very much responsible for whether there are rigid class distinctions among the dancers—principal dancers, semi-soloists, the corps de ballet—or whether all dancers are treated without special distinction, one day performing as a principal dancer, the next as a member of the corps de ballet. The director's view of the dancers plays a large part in the kind of environment you will be experiencing, as well as what will be expected of you in the way of actual dancing.

The artistic director may have been a dancer or a choreographer with a major ballet or dance organization, working under one of the great artistic directors/choreographers, and have had the opportunity to experience his and others' choreography. Usually he or she has had a chance at some point actually to rehearse a group of dancers for performance (if not a large company, at least a community group) before undertaking the artistic direction of his or her own company.

The artistic director has to be financially aware; the vision for the company has to coincide with the funds available to support it. The director is responsible to a board of directors who pay for the vision and bringing it to fulfillment. This means, of course, that the board has put some input into the design of the company; running a dance company is not without its own kind of politics and diplomacy. The artistic director often has to act as a fund raiser and administrator, as well as choreographer, director, and teacher. In smaller companies, he or she does everything. In larger companies, there is often a ballet master or mistress who shares some of the responsibility for preparing the dancers, and other assistants for other areas of running the company, as needed.

Be aware, in joining a company, that if the artistic director is having problems in any of the areas for which he or she is responsible, you, the dancer, will be a reflection of those problems. And if the problems don't have a focus and are not moving toward a resolution, you should allow yourself to consider a change. The company has professional obligations toward its dancers, just as dancers do toward the company. Don't be persuaded by hazy promises of help or support for the company coming "soon," and take half pay or a per diem or a layoff when these provisions don't appear in the contract. It is not productive for the dancer to hang around and get a job waiting on tables while the company irons out its difficulties. You would be better advised to look for another dance job, either in the same city or elsewhere.

The Dancer's Look

Young dancers are concerned, especially if they are aiming for a professional career with a major ballet or modern dance company, about whether their "look" is what is wanted by the people who do the hiring—the artistic directors and the choreographers. Even dancers with more modest ambitions have been conditioned to think there are rules about what a dancer's body should look like. Probably, throughout the training period, the question of whether you match up with a hypothetical ideal has been on your mind. But it becomes a real concern when you step outside the security of the classroom and into the competitive world of professional dance.

Let me say again that in this country, there is a place for everyone who wants to dance and who is willing to undertake the training, whether it be for a professional end or for a learning experience. The only absolute prerequisite is flexibility—of body and mind. No one who wants to dance is defeated before he or she starts by hypothetical ideals; the dancer can create new standards.

I am acquainted with a young woman who trained in America, but

With André Prokovsky in *Brahms-Schoenberg Quartet*.

was unable to find a job here. She happened to find a job with a European company and danced abroad for four years. When she returned to the United States, she studied with me for several months, but was dejected about the seeming difficulties still in getting a position here. She ultimately auditioned for a company in the Midwest, and the artistic director fell in love with her look and her dancing. She got the job—and she was six feet tall!

Star quality has nothing to do with height or perfect proportions. It has to do with talent. The perfect dancer doesn't exist for everyone; "perfection" is a matter of taste, of the artistic director's vision and style. Some artistic directors have specialized artistic tastes, and this is an element you must consider in examining companies you want to work with. If you know your look and your ability well, you will also know whether you are setting yourself up for a disappointment if you audition for a company that uses dancers with a totally different look from yours. (Yet it has happened that a dancer's unique look has sparked the interest of an artistic director and inspired him or her to use a dancer quite unlike the rest of the dancers in a company.)

Part of your "look" has to do with the style of your training as much as it has to do with the genetic inheritance that gives a certain shape to the body. For example, training based on the style of the Royal Academy of Dance gives dancers one "look," while training in a school such as the School of American Ballet gives another. The area of the country you come from also helps determine a look—the climate, the nutrition, the tastes of the public. Don't underestimate how much the "ideal" is defined in terms of what the audience of a region is trained to see, and what the dancer, in turn, thinks he or she ought to look like.

Having denied the existence of an ideal "look" for a dancer, I must acknowledge that there is such a thing as a standard dancer's body that can be referred to for convenience if not as absolute truth. Most women ballet dancers are between about five feet four and five feet seven tall; male ballet dancers are somewhat taller, but are usually about five feet nine or five feet ten. (Modern dance seems to attract huge, tall men, and one wishes they would get involved in classical dance to partner the tall women dancers, who add about three inches to their height when on pointe.)

Practically speaking, long legs are sought in women, small or medium-sized heads, and not too much bosom, with no overdeveloped muscles in the thigh or calf. Dancers who happen to have inherited slim bodies with long arms and legs and mobile joints are fortunate. But more important, I think, is the kind of illusion about your body that you create when you dance, and the quality of your movements.

The way you dance and your temperament play a part in your "look" when you audition and perform. I know two fine young women dancers, both about five feet two. When they stand together offstage, they almost look like twins, with similar body proportions and appearance. One, however, works very quietly and delicately, with small movements. The other dances more broadly, covering the stage when she moves. Onstage, she appears to be about three inches taller than the other. Her temperament alters the dynamics of her movement.

I am not tall, only about five feet four, and I'm not even tall-looking offstage. I don't have especially long legs, yet many times people who have seen me dance are surprised to find me so small in comparison to my onstage look. They were sure I was very tall and had long legs. I looked that way because this was the way I loved to move; my dancing reflected the dynamics of both training and personality. My teachers taught me to use every bit of my legs; they helped me to elongate my muscles. As a result, when I danced, it seemed as though my legs came up to my waist. I was able to dance with very tall men without looking small beside them. I could be made to appear tall in the overall tights I was costumed in for some ballets, yet with a tutu and altered dynamics, I could appear to be much smaller.

The awareness of the quality of your movement and the dynamics of your dancing are more important to your "look" than the unalterable aspects of the body you were born with. Even when young, you have to be honest with yourself and accept what you look like and start from there. With the help of your teacher and coach, you can blend technique and illusion to become a dancer who can catch the eye of artistic directors who want to hire the best dancers, not just bodies that happen to fit a preconceived standard.

Getting the Job: Auditioning

One of the ultimate tests for the young dancer who dreams of a dancing career is putting the training on the line in an audition to see if he or she has something that someone will pay for.

If you have a lot of doubts about whether you are ready, don't ask too soon for disappointment. Even if you do believe you're ready to look for a job, there's a good chance you won't be one of the eight or ten dancers chosen out of a hundred or more at an audition on your first or second or third time out. Many factors are involved: the techniques of auditioning, the questions of artistic taste I've just been speaking of, the confidence you have in your abilities (or the lack of it). I've had students leave my classroom and walk into their first audition with absolute confidence, and their preparation has paid off with a job. I've seen others, with excellent technique, become so nervous at the prospect of an audition that they didn't dance up to their abilities. One very capable young woman auditioned for a major dance company she very much wanted to be a part of, but was so nervous at the vast New York audition that she was eliminated early. The same young woman reauditioned in Florida when the company was on tour, and in the more relaxed atmosphere she was chosen immediately by an artistic director who didn't even remember he had previously auditioned her.

After you find out where auditions for a company are being held, and you've made the decision to go, you have to be aware that for all the questions of art and technique and creativity involved in a performing career, you are still going to a "job interview" like any other. You have to be mentally as well as physically prepared. And you have to look your best—as if you're about to go onstage. You don't go to an audition with torn tights and a tattered leotard (yet far too many young dancers do just that). You don't wear red or green in the hope that you'll stand out in a crowd. You don't wear socks on your shoes because your ankles are cold. You don't wear a skirt that covers up the line of the hip and leg—those running the audition will wonder what it is you're trying to hide.

Your clothes must be fresh and clean, and you have to have a smile on your face. It's not easy to have a hundred and fifty other dancers breathing down your neck for the same job, but your anxieties should never be reflected on your face.

Women dancers should wear black leotards and pink tights. If you want to stand out and if you look well in light colors, wear all pink or all white. Since women must be prepared for pointe work, be sure the ribbons and elastics on your shoes are properly sewn and the shoes themselves are in good shape. They must be broken in—hard toe shoes are a sign of a lack of preparation. Your hair must be properly combed so that it doesn't fly in your face when you do a pirouette. Remember that auditioners are looking at the overall line of the body and head, how the dancer will look on stage. Nothing you wear or the style of your hair should cover up the line.

Male dancers wear a standard "uniform": white shirt, and black tights with white socks and black shoes. Hair should be well cut so that it doesn't fly about or disguise the shape of the head. Again—no camouflage, no attempts to stand out through dress.

Be sure you are prepared for any emergency. Your dance bag should have everything you might need to repair ribbons or elastics or ripped seams. Have hair spray and makeup in case it's a long audition, carry extra tights and leotards and shoes, whatever you need to refresh yourself and look neat—and prepared.

Auditions are, I think, somewhat unfair, but they are necessary. A hundred or so dancers gather in a studio where they've never been before, all hoping to get an honest evaluation. Unfortunately, before your technical abilities are considered, you may be eliminated on the basis of the artistic director's ideas of what he or she is looking for. Some certainly will think you are too tall or too small, in spite of what I have said. Some auditioners do prefer blondes (but don't rush out and change your hair color; the next time they may decide they're looking for dark-haired ladies, and you've lost out twice). If you are eliminated because of some preference of the director's about looks, remember this isn't a rejection of you as a person or a dancer. Men and women face similar problems in this respect, but good male dancers are still eagerly sought, especially if they are tall. A man with the necessary technique for a classical or contemporary company will probably get the chance to demonstrate his abilities.

The young women who are asked to stay at a ballet audition will probably be required to go through a barre. The person auditioning the dancers will give a class to warm them up and see how they take instruction. When the group is divided, he or she will see not only what the dancers' technique is like, but also how the individual dancers respond to his voice, and what their deportment is like as they wait their turn.

The auditioner wants to see what kind of a person you are beyond how well you do the steps. There is a difference, for example, between being pushy and aggressive and being sure of yourself. The chemistry I spoke of earlier is evident in everything you do, and the auditioner has only a brief time to make judgments about you. Make that time count.

Twenty years or so ago, a dancer often prepared a variation for a professional audition. Although this is still sometimes true for college auditions, almost invariably you will be expected to do what the choreographer or artistic director asks you to do. He or she wants to see how easily you take instructions and read combinations. Company dancers are expected to learn choreography quickly, and if you are weak in this area, you aren't a good candidate for an opening.

A student dancer may not have much solid stage experience to include on a résumé, but if you have a background of performing with a group in your hometown or elsewhere, do take the time to make up a résumé that you can bring with you to an audition, along with a few recognizable pictures. Some artistic directors accept résumés to put on file. They see a great many dancers at auditions, and while you may not be chosen at that time, it sometimes happens that a chosen dancer is injured or can't appear for some reason. The director may not have an opportunity for further auditions, and will choose you to step in on the basis of the résumé.

It's a good idea to start going to auditions before you are completely ready to work professionally. Auditioning is a highly tense situation, and you need to have the experience to get over the inevitable nervousness. If you get some auditioning experience behind you, you will be more at ease and can concentrate on displaying your technical abilities instead of worrying and wondering about what is expected of you.

Remember to be prepared for anything, ready to project your joy of dancing to the people who may want to hire you. Work on your technique so that you can extend yourself in front of auditioners. Develop a positive attitude and a strong image of yourself as a dancer. All this can contribute as much to getting a job as your technical training.

The people who audition you select the dancers they think they want, but they may have trouble making a final choice to fill the openings available. If you have been promised a call within a couple of weeks with a decision, and a few anxious weeks pass without word, you shouldn't hesitate to call back and inquire.

Of my own experiences with auditioning, two occasions remain especially vivid. The first was my very first audition for a ballet company. I walked in for an audition with Ballet Russe, and Frederic Franklin said, "Do you have a variation?"

I was totally unprepared for the event, and the command struck terror in my heart. But somehow, the panic and the desire to get the job got me dancing a variation. And I was offered a job.

Some years later, when I was dancing with the New York City Ballet, Charlie Chaplin invited me to dance in his film *Limelight*. When I appeared on the set for the first day's shooting of my part, wearing practice clothes as I had been asked to do and fussed over by the studio makeup department, I found that the set was a stage.

"Where the ballerina auditions," Mr. Chaplin told me. "All right," he said, "do it."

I hadn't even done a barre, I'd never heard the music I was to dance to, and at nine-thirty in the morning, I had to choreograph a variation for myself while a distinguished director and crowds of technicians were waiting to start the cameras rolling.

I went back in my mind to that first audition, and pulled out the feelings of anxiety, the urgency, the importance of the moment. The variation I choreographed to the unfamiliar music appeared on the screen the way Mr. Chaplin wanted it.

Nothing, as I have said, is ever wasted experience in dance.

About Contracts

The smaller ballet or dance companies a student dancer might be asked to join will probably be nonunion (the dancers' union is AGMA,

American Guild of Musical Artists), because the pay scales for union companies are generally too high for city or regional companies. AGMA, however, does recognize this situation and understands the smaller financial margins of these companies and those supported by the National Endowment for the Arts or state councils on the arts. The union often considers them apprentice companies, but still professional.

The AGMA contract is thoroughly negotiated and takes all aspects of the professional dancer's employment into consideration. Nonunion contracts, on the other hand, do not necessarily follow any standard, and have to be completely understood by the dancer. The excitement of being offered a contract sometimes clouds important issues that can have a far-reaching effect on the dancer's experience with a small company.

These are some of the many questions you have to have satisfactory answers to before you sign a nonunion contract:

How much will you be paid, and will it be enough to live on in a new city?

How long is the contract for, and what number of professional performances will be required? What is the proportion of performances to rehearsal time? (A thirty-two-week contract, with twelve weeks of performances and twenty of rehearsal, can be very trying on a prepared dancer—who wants to dance.)

Are you being paid to take class from the artistic director or his assistant or do dance demonstrations? How many classes are you required to take, and are you allowed to take outside class if you feel you aren't getting what you need from the company class?

Does the company pay for your transportation to the city where the company is based, and more important, does it pay your way back when the contract is finished?

Are you covered by unemployment insurance under the contract?

Are you supplied with shoes, and if so, how many? (Remember that this is extremely important in terms of expenses. When you are performing, you can't "get by" one extra day with worn pointe shoes the way you might be able to in class; you have to have the shoes when you need them.)

Be sure you don't just sign a contract without knowing exactly what you are committing yourself to in terms of time and money. If you don't understand all the provisions, get clear answers from the company. Often AGMA will be helpful, even to nonunion dancers, in giving an evaluation of the company's reputation for responsibility toward its dancers. The National Association for Regional Ballet, headquartered in New York, also has a great deal of information about ballet companies around the country. Word-of-mouth from other dancers about how they were treated or what the practical application of a contract's terms actually means is helpful. AGMA can give information about when a dancer is entitled to become a union member and be covered by a union contract.

Young dancers, on being offered a contract, may trust too much to the good will of the management, and lack the experience to know that in the world outside the studio, art is very often tempered by business. Financial support for smaller companies can be precarious; fund raising depends a good deal on the abilities of the artistic director to attract contributors as well as government support. The people who run a company want to produce successful dance, but they also want to get the most for their money from their dancers.

Be sure you know what you are getting from a company for what you are giving in return.

10

COPING
WITH THE WORLD

When I was a young dancer, I agreed to dance in Havana for six weeks with Alicia Alonso's company. Fifty-one weeks later, having covered most of Central and South America, I got back to New York.

In Caracas, we found ourselves in the middle of a revolution, locked up in our hotel after six o'clock every night for a week. We used to throw cigarettes to the soldiers manning the armored truck on the street below our windows, and duck from the snipers.

In Cuba, we played outdoors in stadiums for thousands of people—*Giselle, Prince Igor, Swan Lake*. We traveled by bus throughout the country to dance for children in remote schools. We'd get out of the bus at the bridges, because the structures were barely sturdy enough to support the weight of the bus. The driver took the bus across the open slats that bridged the tremendous drop to the river below.

In Lima, Peru, when we were about to leave after three and a half weeks, we got to the airport to find an old, broken-down army plane with engine problems. So it was back to the city, where the group split up until it was time to leave again. I discovered I had no money, and we weren't leaving until the day after—I didn't eat for a day and a half.

In Buenos Aires, we were locked out of our hotel, and my tights and toe shoes were locked in. We went to the theater for the performance anyway, and wore borrowed costumes.

We traveled on trains that kept breaking down, through small villages in Central America where there was no water to drink and the fruit only made you ill.

Our toe shoes kept wearing out, so we wrapped our shoes in brown paper when the tips wore out (I still use brown paper in my shoes).

I wouldn't exchange one moment of the time I spent on that tour for anything in the world. It allowed me to experience a kind of image of myself, doing what I wanted to do—dancing. No matter where I had to go, I was still doing it—and being bitten by mosquitoes, not having enough money to buy shoes or stamps, staying at grubby hotels with worse food. Yet the experience, and the opportunity of learning from an exceptional person who was conscientious and thorough about any ballet we danced, were worth the discomforts and the uncertainties.

The world in which the dancer has to exist isn't made up of just class and rehearsals and performances. There are always those (metaphorical, at least) revolutions and snipers and pockets of poverty to balance out the rewards of dancing.

Thousands of young men and women put themselves in motion every year in pursuit of their dream. So many of them are drawn to New York and its perils and pleasures. Alison Gonzalez came to the city from Massachusetts: "My teacher at the Cambridge School of Ballet always taught us that when we were ready, she would let us go to New York. It's the place to get the best training, if you want to be a really fine dancer, New York is the mecca."

Paula Hughes came from Pennsylvania by way of North Carolina, where she studied for two years: "I came to get a job—everything is centered in New York, all the auditions. It takes money to travel around to the regional auditions, but you can get to them all here."

Heather Hughes reached New York from Hawaii, stopping for two years at the University of Utah as a ballet major: "I hate the fast pace

Professionals on tour.

sometimes, I don't adapt that easily, but I realized that I was going to have to do it if I wanted to stay in New York."

If there is one thing I have learned from these young women, who are my students and about the same age I was when I arrived, eager and hopeful in New York, it is that not much has really changed in thirty years.

"Yes," they all say, "you have to be adaptable, you have to realize that you're in an insecure business, you have to be prepared to work and to give up things to dance, you have to deal with the pace of New York."

Is it worth it? "Yes! Whether I make it in dancing or not."

Paula commented: "I really freaked out my first week in New York. I'd spent those two years in North Carolina, then a month's vacation at home, and the first day in New York, I got a job to support myself and started classes and had to learn to take the bus and the subway. Even though I knew a couple of people at the studio, I always seemed to be going someplace. I didn't have time to talk to anybody. I got so *lonely*."

How do you survive in New York? Alison, Paula, Heather, and the rest learn to cope and to study dance as well. I owe a lot of my information about coping today to what they and others like them were able to contribute on housing, jobs, roommates, friendships, and attitudes, and especially about the necessity of growing up fast as independent people in the big city.

A Job or Not?

I've said that a full schedule of classes, six days a week, is very much like having a full-time job. Ideally, a young dancer should have sufficient financial backing to be able to study without having to work as well. Unfortunately, the ideal is rarely the reality, especially with the rising costs of city living, dance shoes, and classes. Many young dancers have to find work when they come to the city; however, there are several big *buts* involved.

"I worked five shifts a week as a waitress," Paula said. "I thought I could do it, because I'd worked when I was at school. The difference,

I found out fast, was that in North Carolina, working as a waitress, I was home and in bed by midnight. In New York, it was two or three in the morning. I couldn't make it to a ten o'clock class, I sometimes made it to a noon class, and usually to a two o'clock class—and maybe four, but then it was time to go to work again.

"It felt good to know I was supporting myself, a matter of pride that my family didn't have to support me, but I wasn't really enjoying myself. I wasn't doing more than keeping myself in shape; I wasn't dancing or getting anywhere toward my goal. So I had to put aside my pride and say, 'I can't do it,' and ask my parents for help. Now I work some odd jobs to pay for classes and pointe shoes, and they help with the rent."

Heather pointed out that it's very hard to support yourself working as a waitress and dance as well: "I worked a lunch shift, took class in the mornings and afternoons, and I was dead by nine o'clock."

Alison suggested something I very much believe in: "It works out, if you really want it to. You can find someone to lend you money, the way people get loans for college; parents who believe in you will help."

The reality is that the dancer's economic life is not an easy one without outside support, and there is no simple answer. What has to be kept in mind, I think, is that you shouldn't come to a city like New York assuming that you will be able to support yourself completely and take class as well on a full schedule. You *might* be able to work, and at a pace that allows you to dance as much as you wish, and be able to pay for toe shoes and classes, but your initial step into this world ought to be backed up by sufficient financial support so that you have a chance to adjust to the demands of the life you've set for yourself before you try to support yourself.

What kinds of jobs are available? I was fortunate to have a job dancing at the Radio City Music Hall, but the schedule of performances was killing, especially when combined with dance class. Dance jobs nowadays aren't quite so easy to get, with the abundance of talent in a place like New York. Young dancers turn to waitressing, babysitting, typing, part-time jobs in doctors' and dentists' offices, telephone answering services, telephone solicitation, retail sales jobs (especially at holiday time). New York, since it happens to be crowded with young people trying to combine the pursuit of a show business career with work, does have jobs that are geared to erratic schedules, but except for waiting on tables, they don't usually have high pay rates. You have to take this into account—part-time and temporary employees don't usually rate the same pay scales as full-time, permanent employees.

The young people I know who take class and work are unanimous in saying: "Don't come expecting a waitress job if you've never waitressed. They'll know the first day if you're lying, and then you're out."

It may come down to acquiring a marketable skill in your hometown besides dancing before you weave a fantasy about supporting yourself in the city. Even a summer job as a waiter or waitress gives you experience; the ability to type puts you in a position to take temporary office jobs.

Finding a job isn't all that simple, especially one that gives you sufficient time to take class. There are always want ads in newspapers and temporary secretarial agencies, but young dancers say they make part-time job contacts through friends around the studio—one person passes on news of jobs to another. "It pays to know people who know people in the business world," one student said. "You can get referred to places you wouldn't otherwise hear about, and you sort of have a recommendation by coming through friends." School bulletin boards and bulletin boards in laundromats and supermarkets can give temporary or part-time job leads. And you can just go out on the streets and look.

"I started on a street and went into every restaurant I came to and asked for a job," said one dancer who spent several months as a waiter along with taking class. "I finally hit one that needed a waiter—after trying about a dozen places."

Remember that any job which requires you to be on your feet while you work is going to take its toll on your dancing. Your feet are going to hurt. Be aware that you have to balance out the financial profit and the physical debits. Quite a number of young people will work to make as much money as possible so that they can spend a three- or four-month period taking a full schedule of classes.

Heather said: "I finally realized that it was too physically and mentally tiring to work to support myself entirely and take class. And it was as if my whole life was becoming a waitress instead of a dancer. I asked my parents to look on my dancing as if I were going to college, and they agreed to help with support. For my part, I look on dancing as if I were going to a job, and make sure I take at least two classes a day. It's important, I think, to set rules for yourself, especially since you have so much freedom to make decisions about whether to skip class or slack off in other ways."

Remember, then, why you are coming to a city like New York—to train or to audition as a dancer. Understand what your expenses are going to be and know in advance how you are going to meet them. Be realistic about the kind of income you can expect to earn and how much time it is going to take out of your day. Is it going to be possible for you to fit classes into a work schedule? Will you be able to get from job to class easily? (Even in a city with as vast a public transit system as New York's, it can take a good deal of time to travel from one part of the city to another.) If you happen to injure yourself dancing, you may be required to stay off your feet for a couple of weeks. How will that affect your working—especially if you count on the money to pay the rent and buy food? Again, the cost of a year or two of advanced training in a city like New York is a bargain compared to the cost of four years of college. Many parents welcome the savings to them—if the dancer has demonstrated seriousness of purpose and the maturity to assume responsibility for himself or herself.

"I couldn't think of life without dancing," one of my students said. "I could go back to school, I guess, but I'd never be happy, I don't think, if I couldn't be dancing."

I once asked my daughter what she would do if she weren't a dancer. "Whatever it was," she said, "I'd be a failure at it. I'm a dancer."

Living and Loneliness

"One of the things about New York that's hard," said a student who's been in the city for six months, "is getting together with people. Nobody lives near anybody else, you have to take a subway downtown, and you don't want to take the subway back late at night, so you take a cab. That's expensive, so instead you stay home and watch television."

Cutting free of your roots in your hometown and coming to the city mean you have to expect loneliness. Contrary to popular belief, New York (or any big city) isn't a cold and heartless place, but it is full of busy people, preoccupied with surviving just as you are. (Also, in spite of the numbers of newcomers every year, New York is "hometown" to millions who have a network of friends and relationships that isn't necessarily open to people who have just gotten off the plane or the train.)

The studio, then, is the beginning of your network, and it's another valid reason for not studio hopping. You can make friends there with similar interests and problems. One student remarked that people you meet at a studio can be very helpful to a newcomer—"They'll take you aside and set you straight about how things are done." Teachers should be available to answer a young dancer's questions, and I believe that includes not just dance questions, but queries about adjusting to life in the city. For example, parts of New York are as dangerous as reputation would have them, but much of the city is no more or less perilous than any other big city. A newcomer, though, may need advice on where to get an apartment, the kind of neighborhood a job is in, and so forth. The student should feel comfortable about asking the teacher or the administrator of a studio for advice.

New York rents are high, and a good many students choose to share an apartment to split up the rent. There's another good reason to have roommates, and that is to stave off loneliness. The young dancer can end up being isolated in a world of dance and dance alone.

"I love my dance friends," Alison said, "but I live with a girl who is a few years older than I am, and through her, I have a whole different set of friends. I think it's a good idea to be in a situation where you have other people around."

"Even if you don't want to talk," another of my students remarked, "it's good to know there's someone else there. One of my roommates is a dancer too, so I know there's a person around who understands what my life is."

Having a roommate is a good idea, certainly in the early stages of the New York experience. Because there are so many young people coming and going, it is possible to make connections with people who are looking for a second or third roommate, but again, the easiest way to do this is to get to know the other dancers at your studio who can pass on tips about living arrangements.

A young dancer also has to face the question of using free time. "Dancing is such a big part of my life," one young woman said, "that when I have time off, I don't know what to do with myself. New York has so many things to do, but a lot of them take money. There's only so much walking around you can do. So you go home and wash out your tights and watch television until it's time for bed. At least now that I'm living with someone, I have a person around to talk to."

Dancing does absorb a lot of energy and take a good bit of time. Looking after the details of living—especially for those who have left home for the first time—is another big adjustment. But it pays off, in terms of having a satisfying life, if you have made an effort to be a well-rounded person, and not "just" a dancer. This gives you a range of interests to relax with when you have time off from dancing. As one student of mine said: "You've got to have a real life, too, and you can have it, boyfriends and all. You need the emotion you get from real life to bring it out in your dancing. It's not enough to be a great technician if you're a boring person with nothing to say with your dancing."

What Do You Learn?

"New York is real ballet," one young dancer said. It's not that there aren't superb dancers and companies outside New York, great teachers and a full dance experience, but New York is the essence, a concentrated dose of dance, that can't be found anyplace else in the world. It is true of every form of dance, and the experience of living and studying in a city like New York teaches the young dancer a good deal more than a more polished technique. Everything that is acquired goes into making the dancer better able to cope with the world.

You grow up fast. "It ages you," a dancer who's been studying in New York for several years said. "You feel ten years older than you really are."

You learn what is professional and what isn't. "It wasn't until I got to New York that I realized I had a 'suburban look,'" one girl said. "I could do everything, but nothing worked right; it's indefinable, really, but it's the way the body looks, the lack of muscles. And you figure out fast what the right professional look is and work for it."

You learn when to push yourself. "I was so eager to be first in everything, the best grades, the best dancer, and I pushed myself until I injured myself. When you're here, you learn how to gear yourself to what the body can take, because you know if you injure yourself, there are a hundred dancers who can take your place. Just go to an audition, and you see those hundreds of good dancers who want the two or three spaces that are open."

You learn whether you can handle the competition, and the life. "A lot of people can't survive in New York, can't face the competition. They have to come to some decisions about themselves, not just how good they are, but whether they can face the tension of competing."

You learn not to expect miracles. One dancer who's been studying with me for several months said: "No matter how good the teacher is, or how famous he or she was as a performer, you still have to do it yourself. You go to teachers you think have something to give you, but you've got to take it from them. It's wonderful to see someone who was a star standing five feet away teaching you. You think, 'If she could do it, so can I.' But it has to be you, not her, that puts in the work."

You learn to consider your own personality, and to take responsibility. "You find out a lot about yourself, and how to handle the freedom of deciding to go to class or taking time off. You learn not to be intimidated by the people on the street with that chic New York look, and you figure out the tricks of the trade so you have a good feeling about yourself."

You learn to be adaptable, you learn to be prepared. I have said several times that flexibility of mind and body are essential for the dancer. You adapt not only to the possibilities of dance, but also to the circumstances in which you find yourself. And you do it with a positive attitude, taking each experience as something added to the whole person you are. You can't cope if you're going to fight against the tide every step of the way.

And preparation. In the end, dancing is mostly preparation, and you learn what goes into being a prepared dancer by listening and adapting what you hear to your situation. In a competitive and professional atmosphere you learn very quickly, and then you go out to face the successes and failures and possibilities that await you in dance with confidence.

11

HORIZONS OF DANCE

A dancer is always a dancer.

The choices a dancer makes about performing or using his or her dance training in various ways do not alter the basic image that the years of perfecting the instrument have created. Discipline and focus and the passion for dance don't evaporate when the circumstances of a life change, as inevitably they must.

The evening of May 10, 1973, marked an anniversary gala of the New York City Ballet—a festive occasion attended by an audience of ballet lovers who had long supported the company. The evening also marked the announcement of my retirement as a performer from the company I had been associated with for more than twenty years. I had made my decision to retire some months before, although no one outside of my family and Mr. Balanchine knew of it. In the months before the gala, I came to terms with the idea that each time I danced a ballet now, it was among the last times I would be interpreting the wonderful choreography for an audience that had watched and applauded me for two decades. I felt as if those ballets were gifts to myself, danced not with regret, but with the great pleasure of knowing that I was somehow dancing for myself.

Mr. Balanchine's "gift" to the gala and to me was *Cortège Hongrois*, a new ballet he created for me and my partner of many years, Jacques d'Amboise. The most emotional and touching gift turned out to be the way the gala became a homage to me. To the audience, I was going to retire from dancing, but I knew that I was not going to cease to be a dancer. The horizons of dance are limitless. Just as the forms of dance are many and varied, so are the possibilities, if you want to take them and use them.

When the then mayor of New York, John Lindsay, introduced me to the audience at the gala, and I stood in front of the gold curtain of the New York State Theater with my prepared speech, I could scarcely get the words out. How to respond to the concentrated, shining moment of recognition that is the reason dancers perform?

The people in the gala audience were applauding for me, telling me how much they loved me, how much they appreciated what I had tried to do in dance for all those years. I always knew why I danced; I think young dancers realize why they are performing. They are asking people to say "I love you" with their applause and their acceptance. It is the greatest reward for being a dancer, but it need not happen only once in a lifetime or in performance with a world-famous dance company. The satisfactions of a dancer need not even always have to come from performing, although this is an essential experience at some point in a dancer's life.

The conclusion of my performing career was in reality the beginning of a new career in dance—developing a college dance program, bringing dance to children in public schools, and finally teaching young dancers at my studio. I have, in effect, substituted for applause the satisfaction of seeing talented young dancers develop, many of them into professionals who have the same goals I had when I began my career. I am still, however, as much of a dancer as I was at the height of my career; I couldn't imagine my life without dance.

And it pleases me enormously to see what marvelous choices young dancers have today, where I and other dancers of my generation had so few. We had a handful of companies we could aspire to become

Final performance.

members of. Modern dance was still in the process of becoming a force in American dance. Ethnic consciousness had not yet developed to the point where the dance of many cultures was treasured and ultimately transformed into a theatrical experience. The musical comedy theater had not yet seen the possibilities that were shaping the vision of people like Agnes de Mille.

Then, in the course of the past thirty or so years, a renaissance in dance took place which today means that anyone who studies dance with dedication can find an opportunity to perform, if not as a member of a company on a regular basis, certainly on some stage for some audience—for the love and applause that acknowledge the effort to express artistry in dance.

Regional Ballet

The vast opportunities in dance available today are due largely, I think, to the development of the regional ballet movement and to the efforts of the National Association for Regional Ballet.

There have always been young men and young women who have found in themselves the desire to dance I discovered in my mid-teens. What was lacking to make their dreams a realistic possibility was decentralized opportunities for young dancers to dance and audiences to see them perform. Regional ballet removed classical dance from a handful of performance centers such as New York and San Francisco, and encouraged a widespread interest in dance by bringing it to all parts of the country through sponsoring companies and festivals from coast to coast.

Dorothy Alexander, founder of the Atlanta Civic Ballet, was one of the moving forces in establishing and developing the concept of regional ballet festivals across the United States. These, in turn, have generated interest in dance and local ballet companies. Young people thus have the chance to get out of classrooms and share in dance with fine dancers from throughout their region.

The National Association for Regional Ballet, which is a nonprofit organization funded in part by grants from the National Endowment for the Arts and by the Capezio Ballet Makers Foundation, maintains high standards for its hundred or so member companies across the country (divided into five regions: Southeast, Southwest, Pacific, Northeast, and Mid-States). Associate members are individuals who represent another two hundred dance companies of many types. "We serve all dance persuasions," Executive Director Doris Hering has stated. "The word 'ballet' in our title means any form of dance raised to a theatrical level. We do not, however, pretend to be 'all things to all people.' We are concerned with resident companies creating a climate for dance in their home communities.

"Before 1956, American dance companies outside of New York toiled in isolation. That isolation is now met head-on through the annual regional festivals. Companies come together in adjudicated performances and gain much-needed perspective about themselves."

The regional companies are making dance a vital part of the cultural life of the communities in which they exist, and they and the spring festivals give young dancers a kind of performance experience at an early age that simply didn't exist in my learning years. When the student reaches a city like New York for further training, he or she is already stageworthy, with the confidence to audition for major companies if he or she is technically ready.

Yet more and more dancers choose not to leave their regions, or return to their home communities to become a part of the resident company. It has become possible to stretch the horizons of dance and earn a living in dance outside New York.

It is a satisfying alternative for today's dancer to know that it is no longer necessary to choose between aspiring to a major company whose ranks are always crowded, and not having the chance to perform at all. As a member of the Board of Directors of the National Association for Regional Ballet, I have seen how exciting and creative dance is on the regional level. The artistic accomplishments are high, the vitality is equal to anything seen in the major dance centers.

But there's more. It is no longer necessary to have a dance career or performing experience as a member of a large touring company, a life that is somewhat unsettled and even precarious. Instead, it is possible to settle in a community, be a part of a life many dancers prefer, and still have the chance to dance. Doris Hering has pointed out how welcome the resident companies across the country are to dancers: "There is so much opportunity today for dancers in the decentralized resident dance companies. And any dancer ought to feel proud to be in one of them."

I agree. While the New York experience is an adventure in both dancing and learning about yourself as a person, it is only one of several possibilities for the dancer. You can take away so much from what you discover in New York that you can contribute to the community from which you came or to a new community where you choose to settle. If you are a young woman who decides to marry and make your home where your husband's work is, you don't have to feel that your dance life must end because you are no longer in a big city with major dance companies. You can still participate in the dance world if you happen to be in Gainesville or Wilkes-Barre, in Kalamazoo, Santa Barbara, or Oklahoma City. Male dancers, similarly, don't have to feel that their goals must be limited to New York, but rather they can establish roots in a community elsewhere and discover opportunities in dance so that they can develop a continuing career after their performing careers have ended.

Of course, any dancer who is dedicated to his or her art doesn't need my encouragement to aspire to be the best and to dance with the best company. Every dancer dreams of performing with one of the major dance companies and of becoming an international star. Many dancers come from regional ballet centers to just that point. A number of New York companies, for example, are filled with dancers who had their beginnings in regional ballet and the regional dance festivals. But many, many fine dancers have found their comfort and satisfaction in achieving their best far from New York. The applause and the love of the audience are equal, whether you are performing on the stage of the New York State Theater or on a small stage in a distant corner of the United States. For today's dancer, the horizons really are limitless.

Other Opportunities

For the student who is focusing all his or her energies on perfecting the instrument in order to be able to perform, it is almost unthinkable that anything else is possible. This is as it should be, and I have said that the experience of performing for an audience, going out naked, in effect, to be judged and enjoyed, is essential if you want to call yourself a dancer. But if you have had those good beginnings, if you have acquired not only a vocabulary and a technique, but also a habit of mind that sets no limits to what is possible, you cannot be disappointed for long if you achieve something other than "stardom."

My excellent first teacher gave his students that kind of openness of mind about dance and about themselves. I happened to end up performing in New York, but my fellow students from those years include the artistic director of her own dance company in Alberta, a designer of dance clothes for television and theater, and an established performer in Broadway musicals. Mr. Volkoff never made us believe that the only thing we could be was ballerinas; his dance horizons encompassed so much more. He himself not only taught children and the older group of which I was part, but having been an accomplished character dancer and choreographer in his native Russia, did the choreography for the ice skaters of the Toronto Skating Club.

I recall a fellow dancer who worked for a time with me in the New York company and then decided to return home to the West Coast, where she married and raised a family, while continuing to perform occasionally and to teach ballet. Years later, her daughter came to study with me at my studio. She was a young woman with exceptional focus and a strong image of herself as a dancer—a gift, in part, from her mother.

We give back to dance what we have gained in so many ways. I see my own daughter dancing now not because I expected it of her, but because we as her parents allowed her the chance to discover dance when she expressed an interest in learning. Yet I had gained so much from dance that I knew that however far she wanted to extend the experience, she too would gain.

I see young men and women making judgments about themselves and their abilities and altering their focus to different kinds of dance—expressions of ethnic or racial consciousness that are both brilliant theatrical dance and supports for a special kind of self-image. I have seen trained dancers enter the world of theatrical dance as musical comedy performers and extend their training beyond ballet, modern, and jazz dance to singing (so many Broadway casting notices call for "dancers who can sing"). Today, not only is choreography an exciting aspect of the world of dance, with all those hundreds of regional companies eager for new ballets, but the management of dance companies, the design of dance productions, and the costuming of dancers are all areas where trained dancers can find careers if they do not choose to perform or if, for some reason, they are unable to meet the demands of a stage career.

I have found great satisfaction in teaching, and many other former performers have done so as well. Young dancers may not have the range of experience and perception necessary to teach advanced students, but as dance has become a greater part of our cultural life, many trained dancers have found a profession in sharing their knowledge with children, in dance therapy for the physically and mentally disabled, in exercise programs, in any number of areas. The limits are set only by your imagination.

The important thing, I think, is that the climate is now so favorable for a life in dance, thanks to the efforts of the National Association for Regional Ballet, to the growing awareness of the public of the value of dance, and to the widespread appreciation for this wonderful creative art form.

I began by saying I couldn't live without dancing. Almost every dedicated dancer feels the same way, but today we are fortunate in having audiences who also know and love dance. This is what gives dancers the opportunity to be dancers—this and the desire that gives a dancer the dream and the will to shape the instrument and *to dance*.

APPENDIX

The National Association for Regional Ballet is the service organization for decentralized resident dance companies in the United States and Canada (some one hundred companies, with many more dance companies represented by individuals who are associate members of the association).

Each member company consists of at least twelve dancers, had been incorporated for at least one year before applying for membership, and had given at least one performance for a paying public before being admitted to membership. The Professional Wing consists of companies that have a minimum number of paid dancers under contract for a certain number of weeks per year and give a stipulated number of performances, among other criteria.

Major Company status is the highest accolade the National Association for Regional Ballet bestows upon its members. According to the association, "It is a distinction that bears the responsibility the NARB stands for and the ballet-going public expects."

The criteria by which the companies are judged are these:

1. Quality of training
2. Range and quality of performance
3. Artistic presentation
4. Development of male dancers
5. Service to the community of residence as well as to the national association

6. Ethical behavior toward other companies and toward the community at large

For the 1979–1980 season, for example, seven companies were selected as NARB Major Companies. They show the wide geographical range of the companies that make up the membership of the national association:

The Atlanta Ballet (1404 Spring Street NW, Atlanta, Georgia 30610; Robert Barnett, artistic director), the oldest ballet company in the United States and a charter member of the NARB Professional Wing.

Ballet Pacifica (1863 South Coast Highway, Laguna Beach, California 92651; Lila Zali, artistic director).

The Dayton Ballet (150 North Main Street, Dayton, Ohio 45402; Josephine Schwarz, artistic adviser; Bess Saylor and Jon Rodriguez, associate directors), the second oldest regional company in the United States and a member of the Professional Wing.

Greater Houston Civic Ballet (9902 Long Point Road, Houston, Texas 77055; Margo Marshall, artistic director; Christine Lidvall, associate director).

The Louisville Ballet (200 East Oak Street, Louisville, Kentucky 40508; Alun Jones, artistic director), a charter member of the Professional Wing.

The Princeton Ballet (262 Alexander Street, Princeton, New Jersey 08540; Audree Estey, artistic director; Jane Miller Gifford and Barbara Sandonato, associate directors), which has been in existence for more than twenty years.

Tulsa Ballet Theatre (5414 South Gillette Street, Tulsa, Oklahoma 74105; Moscelyne Larkin and Roman Jasinski, artistic directors).

Information about the National Association for Regional Ballet, its member companies and services (placement, regional festivals, choreography conferences, National Choreography Plan, Board Member Handbook, *Dance/America*, the official publication of NARB, and Set and Costume Rental Service) may be obtained from the association, 1860 Broadway, New York, New York 10023.

For twenty-eight years, Melissa Hayden was a leading ballerina with the New York City Ballet (1949–73) and American Ballet Theatre (1945–47; 1953–54). Following her retirement from the stage in 1973, she spent three years teaching dance at the college level as an artist-in-residence and director of ballet. Today she heads Melissa Hayden, Inc., her dance studio in New York City.

INDEX